COMMITMENT AND COMMEMORATION

Jews, Christians, Muslims in Dialogue

Edited by
André LaCocque

Exploration Press, Chicago

"The Memory of Commitment"
(Abraham Heschel, *God in Search. . .*, p. 212)

Printed in the United States of America.

Exploration Press
Chicago Theological Seminary
5757 University Avenue
Chicago, Illinois 60637

ISBN: 0-913552-54-2

Library of Congress Catalog Card Number: 93-72787

Table of Contents

Introduction

Jews, Christians, and Muslims

These last few years, the *Center for Jewish-Christian Studies of the Chicago Theological Seminary* has organized dialogical conferences with Jewish, Christian, and Muslim speakers. Even today, such encounters between the three Abrahamic faiths are all too rare while the need for such conversations constantly waxes. It is thus with a feeling of pride and hope that we present today to our readers the proceedings of some of the past conferences, first landmark on the road to further encounters.

In this volume, thus, the reader will find a selection of the proceedings of the CJCS conferences with Muslim participation. The latter has added an important dimension to the Jewish-Christian dialogue, that we have initiated much earlier. On that score, three points appear to me to be particularly significant:

First, as can be expected by Jews and Christians, who already have a large experience of that fact within their respective traditions, there is in Islam a yawning hiatus between the doctrine of the Qur'an on the one hand, and its subsequent interpretations, on the other. A fundamental problem arises here whether what is decisive is the point of departure, or the point of "arrival?" As the main characteristic of Jewish, Christian, and Muslim religions is that they all claim to be "revealed," meaning that they have foundational and inspired Scriptures of their own, the three of them dispose of given criteria or touchstones to "check and balance" their subsequent traditions. There is therefore a healthy back and forth internal movement between the past and the present historical poles that seems to be indispensable for Jews, Christians and Muslim alike. True, the parallel between the three does not necessarily go very far, for there are various degrees in the congruity of "validating" the historical development against its scriptural origin. Even within the same confession, for that matter, there are fluctuations. It is clear that Christian Protestants are using their Scriptures more anxiously than do Christian Catholics, for instance. Be that as it may, there obtains in Judaism, Christianity, and Islam, a dialectical relationship between what can be called the tree and its branches.

A second point of profound significance, in my opinion, is the universalistic character of Judaism, Christianity, and Islam. All three admit converts from all races, from all walks of society, from all spiritual horizons. Their common monotheism brings them naturally to the necessary conclusion that the world created by God is also one world. Such a belief is fundamental and yields immeasurable consequences. It certainly eventuates ontologically in an egalitarian conception of the human race. As everyone is a potential Jew/Christian/Muslim, it means that no one can be categorized as genetically inferior. The God One not only took the care of creating him/her, but He did so with the same love and the same expectation as with the creation of the Jew/the Christian/the Muslim. Ethically, it also means that, as regards prescriptival standards, there are neither "primitives" nor "civilized." Everyone is under the sacred obligation of being "human." Expressed in reversed order, to be human does entail specific obligations that no one can transgress without retrograding to a sub-human state of animality. In that respect, foundational texts abound in Judeo-Christianity. I mention only the example of Amos 1-2. In the Qur'an, one will refer to Ernest Hamilton's article here on "The Qur'an and the Descendants of Korah."

More controversial is a further aspect of universalisim. It implies that the world will reach its perfection/unity, and respond in full to its very raison d'être, when all nations will come to Mt. Zion and receive (accept) the Torah as Moses received it on Mt. Sinai (Isa. 2.2-4 = Mi 4.1-3)/when all nations will confess that Jesus Christ is Savior/when all humans will become Muslims! — Clearly, this is the point where the way "trifurcates." It is true that, speaking of Judaism and Christianity and their respective eschatologies, Edmond Fleg once expressed the liberating possiblity that the Messiah expected by Jews, and the Parousia expected by Christians, would be the same event. From that perspective, allowing as it does that human limitations and "impossibilities" might transpire only in the realm of historical finitude, there is no impassable hurdle to completing Fleg's thought with the hope that, at that blessed time of the coming of the Christian and Jewish Messiah, all of humanity will be Muslim!

Of course, this is only speculation. But speculation for the future made in faith, love, and hope, may prove to be constructive and creative for the present. The object and objective of dialogue is, after all, the actual willingness on the part of the dialogists to be dis-oriented and re-oriented by the other(s). To take a example to the contrary, it is evident that a Christian restrictive understanding of Jesus' declaration according to which, "no one comes to the Father [God], but through me," would thwart any constructive dialogue with non-Christians. Another interpretation of the Johannine Jesus' statement is necessary: all those who in the whole world and throughout history accede to the father, it is through me [Christ] that they have that access. Where there is access to God, there is mysteriously Christ... Jesus' declaration is a statement of realized eschatology, not of dogmatic exclusivism.

Thus, dialogue between the three Abrahamic faiths is conditioned by their eschtologies. The world's unity under the God One, and humanity's implementation of God's will as revealed by, and sometimes incarnate in, Moses, or Jesus, or Mohammad, is an eschatological hope and expectation. Meanwhile, however, the eschaton is reflected in the historical present, or else is a perfunctory insignificant expectation of a "pie in the sky." Consequently, the doctrine must take that reality in consideration and explain its significance. *Judaism* is again on that score somewhat at odds with the other two religious traditions. It teaches that the whole of humanity is creationally monotheistic (see Genesis 1-11) and is as a whole in convenantal realtionship with God (see Genesis 6-8). The divine demands from humanity are very limited and basic, essentially to refrain from spilling and/or consuming blood. So, although conversion to Judaism is a real option offered to all, such conversion is unnecessary, as it gains no easier or speedier access to God. It is certainly no condition for salvation. Among the "nations," there are "righteous of the world," and they are, like any faithful Jew, the delight of God.

Islam on the other hand, is, at least at times, more aggressively missionary, as is also *Christianity*, with ambivalence as to the real merit before God of being a Jew or a Christian (alternatively: of being a Jew or a Muslim). But, as is normal in any "doctrine of life," there are in both families on that issue a great variety of aspects and approaches. (So, by the way, are there differences in Jewish attitudes toward non-Jews. Sometimes, say the Rabbis [on Psalm 80.13], nations are like an "hippopotamus" [inoffensive], sometimes like a "boar" [harmful], and one must deal with them accordingly). Here, suffice it to highlight the Islamic doctrine of the plurality of prophets to the different nations of the world. Islam follows the instructions of the great prophet Mohammad, but to all nations God has sent prophets; to the Jews, Moses, and to the Christians, Jesus. To this must be added the Qur'anic use of the term "believers" which, at times, designates not only the Muslims proper, but all theists. Similarly, "idolaters" or "ingrates" may be applied equally to non-Muslims and to Muslims. — There is therefore a fundamentally tolerant spirit inherent to Islam, especially vis-à-vis the other two monotheistic religions.

I see a third striking point of convergence of the three Abrahamic traditions in the all-important issue of the role of woman. All three religions must tackle this which has always been a problem respectively in Judaism/Christianity/and Islam. Elsewhere, I have expressed my conviction that the place allotted to women in any given society or organizaton is the most reliable barometer, so the speak, indicating the degree of love, justice, liberty, and peace, reached by that society. Other societal issues are important, but none of them supersedes that one. Now, I for one have found particularly moving how similar are the *desiderata* and the suggestions for improvement of the situation among the three kin groups, not in the name of any theoretical equalitarian point of view, but in the name of religious authenticity. To a certain extent, although the modes of discourse are diverse, it makes no essential difference whether the voice is Muslim, Jewish, or Christian. I see in this harmony a sure token of a fundamental unity of understanding as regards justice and liberty in the Abrahamic faiths.

It is on that note that I'd like to conclude. The following contributions by Jewish, Christian, and Muslim scholars, are remarkable from several points of view. One common characteristic stands out, however: their total, genuine, and courageous *honesty*. I take pride to present to this book's readership the proceedings of CJCS conferences at the Chicago Theological Seminary in the recent years.

JUNE 1993
ANDRÉ LACOCQUE

Part I

The Way of Commitment

In Memoriam of Dr. Fazlur Rahman

Professor Fazlur Rahman died shortly after delivering his lecture that appears here below. We begin this volume with an *In Memoriam* signed by Dr. William A. Bijlefeld, another contributor to this book.

Fazlur Rahman, undoubtedly one of the most prominent — and at times in some circles one of the most controversial — Islamic scholars of our time passed away in Chicago on July 26, 1988.

Born in Seraisaleh, Pakistan, on September 21, 1919, Fazlur Rahman received his B.A. and M.A. degrees from the University of Punjab, in 1940 and 1942 respectively, and his D.Phil. from Oxford University in 1950. His distinguished academic career included periods of service at the University of Durham, England (Lecturer, 1950-1958), the Institute of Islamic Studies, McGill Univerity, Montreal, Canada (Associate Professor, 1958-1961), the Islamic Research Institute in Karachi, Pakistan (Visiting Professor, 1961), and the Islamic Research Institute in Islamabad, Pakistan (Director, 1962-1968). In 1969 he came to the U.S.A., taught for a short period as Visiting Professor at U.C.L.A., and found his place for the next two decades at the University of Chicago, where he was Professor of Islamic Thought from 1969 onward. His outstanding contribution to the life of the University was recognized in 1986 when he was honored by the appointment as the Harold H. Swift Distinguished Service Professor.

The impressively wide span of his academic interests and the significance of his many contributions to various aspects of the study of Islam have been acknowledged widely and will, I trust, continue to be discussed and assessed from several perspectives in the years ahead. Throughout his career Fazlur Rahman addressed a number of highly critical and controversial issues, eliciting strong reactions of grateful consent and shocked disagreement. More than once he pointed with a deep sense of urgency to the task to "elaborate an Islamic metaphysics on the basis of the Qur'ãn" as a condition and prerequisite for the much needed "Islamizing of the several fields of learning." He never tired of explicating in different contexts what was invloved in this "systematic interpretation of the Qur'ãn." One illustration is the way he summarized his conclusions of Qur'anic legislation:

> In building any genuine and viable Islamic set of laws and institutions, there has to be a twofold movement: First one must move from the concrete case treatments of the Qur'ãn — taking the necessary and relevant social conditions of that time into account — to the general principles upon which the entire teaching converges. Second, from this general level there must be a movement back to specific legislation, taking into account the necessary and relevant social conditions now obtaining (*Islam and Modernity*, 1982, p. 20).

At several occasions he stressed the need to distinguish between normative Islam and historical Islam (as he distinguished historic from normative Christianity in "Islam's Attitude towards Judaism," M.W., 72 (1982), 10), and his criticism of the present state of affairs in much of the Muslim world ("how to recover Islam from the debris of history") was as sharply articulated as his firm belief in Islam's central task: "to construct a social order on a viable ethical basis," a task for which Muslims had to rediscover "the real Islam, ...concretely ever-present in the Qur'ãn and its ethical principles," not only for their own sake, but "for the benefit of all mankind" ("Islam: Challenges and Opportunities," in Alford T. Welch and Pierre Cachia, eds., *Islam; Past Influence and Present Challenge*, 1979, pp. 315-30). To his most frequently quoted statements belong perhaps the words about the Qur'ãn in his *Islam*, 1966, p. 31, on the need to affirm "both the Qur'ãn is entirely the Word of God and, in an ordinary sense, also entirely the word of Muhammad". And almost anyone dealing with the issue of religious pluralism from the Qur'anic perspective has at one time or another made reference to one of the appendices in his *Major Themes of the Qur'ãn*, 1980, pp. 162-70: "The People of the Book and Diversity of 'Religions'."

But even a simple listing of ideas and publications of Fazlur Raham that have reached much wider circles of readers than those more or less professionally involved in Islamic Studies would go far beyond the scope of this obituary. To conclude this "In Memoriam" it seems appropriate, however, to give one more quotation, this time from his *Health and Medicine in the Islamic Tradition*, 1987, p. 127:

> If ... men and women can develop *tawaã* in this life and see themselves for what they really are, there *will be no need for the Day of Judgment*, for every moment of life will be the Hour of Judgment.
>
> Death for the Qur'an, then, is a mere link or a passage between two segments of a continuous life ... (followed by S. al-Zumar [39]:42).

In more than one way life and work of Fazlur Rahman *do* continue, by the grace of God.

WILLEM A. BIJLEFELD

The Muslim World, LXXIX, 1 (1989), pp. 80-81.
Reprinted here with kind permission of *The Muslim World*.

I

Meet Dr. Fazlur Rahman

BY ANDRÉ LACOCQUE

The Prophet Muhammad had a liberal attitude toward *bona fide* Jews and Christians whom he acknowledged as the righteous among the nations. Anyone familiar with rabbinic Judaism recognizes here a perfect parallel with the attitude of many rabbis of old as well as of today regarding the so-called "righteous of the nations" in whose number all of the Muslims and Christians in this room hope to be.

Many Christians, however, it must be confessed have historically been a lot more reluctant in sharing a similarly generous, broad-minded, and relaxed stance vis-à-vis anyone who is not a Christian. It is within the vocation of the Center for Jewish-Christian Studies to wholeheartedly espouse the rabbis' and Muhammad's joyful insight. No one, we believe, can speak of "God's people" in an exclusivistic way. God's people transcends the institutional, national, racial, and confessional limits. There are in that innumerable army of which speak Ezekiel, the Gospel and the Qur'an, Jews and Christians and Muslims, to follow a chronological order, and still many others. Such a conference as it takes place today had to occur at some point in the developmental growth of the Center for Jewish-Christian Studies. Because of the impossibility of realizing this trancendent reality of God's people without recognizing its multifaceted pluralism, a systematic ignorance of one of the members of the Abrahamic faith would amount to some sort of heresy, taking the term in its etymological meaning.

Furthermore, in a world of polarized interests, of paradoxical regionalisms, particularisms, coteries of all kinds, any affirmation of globalism comes as a welcome relief. It is absolutely out of the question that we today get into political issues, such as the tragic confrontations in the Middle East and elsewhere. Whatever may be our personal convicitons in this regard, it must be clear that in all consciousness, the organization of this conference is by itself a message of peace. I hereby invite everyone present to keep it this way. No political question from the floor will be honored. This conference is meant as an introduction into Islam for people who want to know more about it. The lecturers gathered for this event are amongst the greatest specialists in the field. Before I say a few words about them, I want here to express the profound gratitude of the Center for Jewish-Christian Studies and of the Chicago Theological Seminary as a whole toward these scholars whose dedication to scholarship, and for some of them at least, to Islam, have prevailed over all considerations, such as a just financial compensation for sharing with us their science. The Center for Jewish- Christian Studies disposes of extremely limited means, and in front of this distinguished panel it makes us in the Center both somewhat ashamed but also proud of their disinterestedness. This dialogue is put under the sign of genuineness in our efforts to understand and to be edified. It is to be conducted in a spirit of respect, love, and awe.

The first of our speakers this morning is Dr. Fazlur Rahman, professor at the Oriental Institute. Dr. Rahman was born in Sept. 21, 1919 in Pakistan. He got his M.A. degree from Punjab University, Lahore in 1942 with First Class in Arabic, and was a research student in the Punjab University from 1942 to 1946. He received his Ph.D. degree at Oxford, England in 1949 with a thesis on Avicenna's psychology. He was Lecturer in Persian Studies and Islamic Philosophy at Durham University, England, from 1950 to 1958, and Associate Professor, Institute of Islamic Studies, McGill University, Montreal, 1958 to 1961, Visiting Professor, Central Institute of Islamic Research, Pakistan, 1961 to 1962, and its Director from 1962 to 1968. Visiting Professor at U.C.L.A., spring term 1969. He was Professor at the University of Chicago from 1969 to 1986, and Howard Swift Distinguished Service Professor of Islamic Thought from 1966 to the present at the same university. He attended many international conferences including the World Muslim League at Mecca, visited Indonesia at the invitation of the government in the summer 1985 to "assess the situation of Islam" there and advise higher Islamic education. He was also consultant to the state Dept. in this country, in the White House during the '79 to '80 years. He received lately the De La Vida Award in Islamic Studies in 83, and he currently teaches and conferences on ethics and Islam. He has written a great number of books, book reviews, and articles. Let me just at random pick up a title or two — I see *Avicenna's Psychology*, of course, which was his Ph.D. dissertation, *Prophecy in Islam*, 1968; *Islamic Methodology in History*, 1965; *Islam*, 1967; *The Spirit of Islam*, 1984; *Major Themes of the Qur'an*; *Islam and Modernity*; *Islam and Health Medicine: Revival and Revival and Reform in Islam.* And, as I said earlier he made many, many other contributions, scholarly contributions which would be too long to just mention here.

Dr. Rahman we are very much indebted to your coming to us this morning. We thank you, we are your disciples.

II

Muhammad and the Qur'an

BY FAZLUR RAHMAN

First of all, I wish to congratulate the Center for Jewish-Christian Studies for having brought to the conference of today this dialogue for mutual constructive understanding and, secondly, let me express how honored I feel to have been asked to address this conference on the subject of Muhammad and the Qur'ãn.

I shall broadly divide this subject into three topics. First, I shall say some words about Muhammad and the Qur'ãn, that is, his relationship to the Qur'ãn, which itself is, of course, a multifaceted problem, but I shall try to indicate the more important of them. Second, I shall say a few words about the manner of revelation, that is, how, according to the Qur'ãn, the Qur'ãn was communicated to the Prophet Muhammad (pbuh). And third, the matter of revelation — what was conveyed to the Prophet. This third topic, is of course, extremely important because it encompasses the entirety of the Qur'ãn, the Qur'anic message, but I shall try to draw our attention to certain foundational concepts of the God-man relationship.

The first topic, or sub-topic, is the fact of revelation. The fact of revelation is treated in the Qur'ãn in several places and in various ways. That the Qur'ãn came from a source that was not the Prophet himself is a very basic contention of the Qur'ãn. In one verse, the Qur'ãn says, "Do these people say: He (Muhammad) has invented it (the Qur'ãn)?" (10:38), and in another it says, "If God so willed, He could seal up your heart" (42:24). There will be no revelation then. It is not up to Muhammad to bring revelation; it is God who sends revelation when He thinks revelation is needed. Throughout the Qur'ãn, the evidence is overwhelming that the Prophet himself stood under the obligation of the Qur'ãn. There's a verse in the Qur'ãn, for instance, which says, "If We had sent down this Qur'ãn upon a mountain, you (O Muhammad), would have seen it humbled, rent asunder by the fear of God" (59:21). I don't know of any author in the world whose heart was so much under the weight of a book he himself wrote. There are numerous indications, as I have stated, that the source of the Qur'ãn lay somewhere outside the Prophet. I don't think we need to elaborate on this any further. There are, of course, questions arising as to what was the source, the actual source of the Qur'anic revelation; and, I think, there, the best course is to believe what the Qur'ãn says, that it is from God. What reason can there be not to believe the Qur'ãn?

The second topic is the manner of revelation. The manner of revelation of the Qur'ãn is also spelled out in the Qur'ãn in great detail. I have mentioned one verse here, already, which says to Muhammad (pbuh) that "if God so willed, He could seal up your heart" (42:24); there will be no more revelation. This shows us, clearly, that the Prophet's consciousness was invaded from time to time, when the opportunity for it arose, by some force and that this force definitely came from his heart. It came through his heart — "We shall seal up your heart" — God says to the Prophet. Elsewhere, also, the Qur'ãn says to the Prophet, that this Qur'ãn is "brought down upon your heart, that you may be (one) of the warners" (26:194). So these verses conclusively show that the Qur'ãn was not the work of the Prophet's mind, and, secondly, that nonetheless the Qur'ãn came to his heart. The Qur'ãn pushed so forcefully through his heart that immediately it got clothed in words. I'm reminded of a sentence in the late Professor Hocking's book, *The Meaning of God in Human Experience*, where, talking about religious experience, one has a powerful feeling which then propels itself automatically into an idea, and the idea expresses itself automatically in words. This is the revelation, or the revelatory experience par excellence.

I think that the relationship between the Prophet's personality and the revelation has been so confused both by Muslims and by non-Muslims that, although the picture is very clear from the Qur'ãn, people have tried to overlay it with certain concepts that are foreign to the Qur'ãn. I am not here, of course, talking about non-Muslims because until recently, relatively recently, for them the Qur'ãn was a concoction of the Prophet. Just as the Meccans accused him of concocting the Qur'ãn, so did the West. It is relatively recently that the Western scholars have begun to appreciate the revealed quality of the Qur'ãn and its luminous character. Somewhere early in the career of the community, probably in order to avoid the suspicion that the Qur'ãn came from the Prophet himself, the Muslims made the Angel Gabriel the agent of revelation, who is sometimes called "Jabriel" in the Qur'ãn, but is more frequently called "al-ruh alamin," that is, "the trusted spirit" (26:193). Because of this anxiety, they made all sorts of theological efforts to show Gabriel not only as the source of the Qur'ãn extrinsic to the Prophet, (outside of the Prophet), but that the actual process of revelation was also outside him. So they tried to portray the angel of revelation, the "trusted spirit," as some kind of a being who came from the outside and gave to the Prophet messages from God, more or less in the same manner as the postman hands you over your mail. And this has, this mechanical sort of picture has, done a lot of damage to a real understanding of the relationship between the person of the Prophet and the Qur'ãn.

For several other reasons, Muslims, or the majority of them, actually a vast majority of them, came to equate the *Sunna* of the Prophet, that is, the Prophet's own words and deeds through which he acted out the Qur'anic message, as something revealed, almost like the Qur'ãn. Others, most recently in their reaction to this doctrine, have gone to the extreme of trying to hold that all the Prophet came to do was to deliver the Qur'ãn, exactly like an oracle, and that otherwise, the Qur'ãn had nothing to do with his personality. These people, the so-called "Modernists," I think, are doing, perhaps in some ways greater injustice to the Qur'ãn and the Prophet than the holders of the first view. I have chosen to elaborate a little on this question because the Muslims have really to reconstitute, almost from scratch, the Qur'anic view of how the Qur'anic revelation was related to the Prophet. We know very well that the Prophet had certain problems on his mind that tormented him, that drove him to the cave of Hera to contemplate and pray to God for a solution, and that it is then that the *wahy*, the divine guidance, burst upon him. How can all this happen in a vacuum?

Now let me try to say a little about the third topic, which is the content of the Qur'anic message — the matter of revelation. The Qur'ãn touches upon all the questions that a human being individually and collectively faces, and it is in this sense that the Qur'ãn says that the Qur'ãn has everything in it. However, the basic character of the Qur'anic message, I believe, is that it has come to teach man how to approach God, how to communicate with God through prayers and other good acts, but this approach to God is constantly in a way preparatory for man to approach other men — how man must behave, individually and collectively. There's a verse where the Qur'ãn says, "There is no secret meeting of three but He is their fourth, nor of five but he is their sixth, nor of less than that or more but He is with them wheresoever they may be" (58:7). Wherever there is more than one human being, God enters into their midst. This is, I believe, what the Qur'ãn has come to teach — how to regulate man's approach to man.

It is for this reason that the Qur'ãn talks so repeatedly so and insistently of the quality of the human act. The human act is unique. A donkey also acts. When it's hungry, it tries to find food, eat food, and it does various things; it sleeps. Man also does these things, but there's a quality to man's act which the donkey's actions don't possess, and they are not supposed to possess. It is this quality that the Qur'ãn calls "the weight of an action" (*al-wazn*, 7:8; 18:105; 101:6).

And the Qur'ãn is insistent that actions not only have their weight, but they will be weighed. These actions will be weighed in order for man to face the meaning of those actions. A human being is not the kind of creature or a being who, when he or she produces his or her action, the action goes away. No, the meaning of the action remains, and it is this meaning which is its weight. You see, the Meccans used to weigh commodities, (it was a trading community); they used to weigh gold and silver, and it is in their language that the Qur'ãn says to them, "those whose scales are heavy (with good works), they are the successful. And those whose scales are light are those who lose their souls, in hell abiding" (23:102-103). Their deeds will be weighed. I'm sure most of them looked askance at the Qur'anic statements and said, How can deeds be weighed? And, I think, many today would wonder how deeds can be weighed, but the Qur'ãn insists that all human actions are transitive; they have a meaning which does not remain limited to the doer, to the actor. And, unless man basically appreciates this fact, there is no way that his behavior can be put on the right track.

The Qur'ãn graphically portrays how, in the final analysis, at the end (*alyawn al'ãkhir*, 2:8), when all is said and done, how at the end, people who never attach any importance to what they are doing will feel at that hour when they face the consequences or the meaning of their actions. Their actions will have no substance. They will be like motes in the air — no weight at all. Or their actions will be like ashes, which will be borne by a hard wind, they will all be scattered around, there will be nothing left to see. And so the Qur'ãn invites man to do consequential actions — actions that will be meaningful for humankind. Remember, whenever two of us are there, God is there. This means that whatever I do, think about, and do to my fellow human beings, God takes notice of that, and even in the utmost privacy of my heart, God is there. God intervenes between man and his own action.

You see, this is why God is needed. Without God, human conduct just cannot remain on the right track. We have seen the workings of humanism in its various form, we have seen godless humanism, we have seen humanism with some sort of God, and we now realize that unless there is a God who is here and now, man cannot remain on the right track; he must go wrong. Of course, there have been humanisms earlier in history, and ours is not the only age that has experienced humanism. By humanism I mean, here, that there is no spiritual presence of force; there is no moral presence or force except you and me. This is what I call humanism in this context. Oh, there has been humanism before, as I have said. There was the period of Greek enlightenment, when people tried to explain away their religious ideas and symbols as some sort of metaphors — if you read Cicero's *De Natura Deorum*. Of course, this doesn't mean that those plurality of gods of the Greeks was a correct representation of religion. We need not say that, and yet, when that enlightenment came, it swept away the effect of the religious meaning of life and it left man with the barest sensible experience that he had. And, then, we saw the result of that also.

So, both liberalism and humanism are important, you see. Humanism, in a sense, is extremely important because I have said that the experience of God exists, not primarily per se to experience God, but in order to correct one's relationship with an experience of man. So, in this sense, humanism is there, it is the center. But this humanism cannot be kept in its true form without feeling the presense of — I don't want to use the word, "without believing" — without feeling the presence of another force that is beyond you and beyond me, and under whose eyes, if you like, we all stand. The Qur'ãn, therefore, brings the idea of accountability of man, both individually and collectively, in the center of religion.

Further, the Qur'ãn claims that the tenets it is upholding, such as belief in God, or I should say, feeling of God, and its meaning, His meaning for life and for the future of man are the tenets that all prophets before Muhammad had been upholding. It then constructs a spiritual history of mankind where all prophets have been contributing to this theme. It, therefore, declares that man's primordial experience of religion is a valid experience.

The truth did not come for the first time with Muhammad. It did not come for the first time with Abraham. It came for the first time with the advent of man. And, therefore, all human beings, all nations, and all countries have been recipients of divine guidance. The Qur'ãn tells us that "there is not a nation but a warner has passed among them" (35:24), and that "mankind were one community, and God sent (unto them) prophets as bearers of good tidings and as warners, and revealed therewith the Scripture with the truth that it might judge between mankind concerning that wherein they differed" (2:213). There has been no cultural groupings in which some guide divinely inspired has not appeared. Therefore, religious guidance is a part of human life. It is there. Of course, man has grown up over millennia and centuries. This is also what the Qur'ãn affirms. And, therefore, today's people cannot be judged by the standards of divine guidance that was sent thousands of years ago, even though the basic truth remains the same. This is the contention of the Qur'ãn. There is, then, some kind of a development in history. This development cannot be lost sight of. This is why the Qur'ãn says that on the Day of Judgement, God will bring out of each community its witnesses (4:41, 49), that is, its divinely sent or divinely inspired guides.

Then, of course, there are other things the Qur'ãn brings in: that people somehow, after the initial message, misconstrue their message and fight among themselves. This is an act which the Qur'ãn laments ceaselessly, from the beginning to the end. People begin to quarrel among themselves, so that each group regards what it possesses itself as the truth. And they refuse to look at their neighbor's truth. The Qur'ãn says, "And lo! this your religion is one religion and I am your Lord, so keep your duty unto Me. But they (mankind) have broken their religion among them into sects, each sect rejoicing in it tenets" (23:52-53). Note that the Qur'ãn does not use the word community, *umma,* as it does in the verse I have already quoted (2:213), but sect, *hizb.* These sects, subgroups, these self-constituted and self-proclaimed men of religion, these cliques, the Qur'ãn says, are very happy in what each of them has. One sect does not care to know what the other has. And it is for this reason that the Qur'ãn stresses unity of religion, because it believes that, fundamentally, religion is a unity. And it is a unifying force because God is one. God, who has sent this guidance, is one.

The Qur'ãn does not, of course, say that people may not differ. People do differ, but it is also sure that much of the differences of opinion is not well-intentioned, it is not well-meant. And the Qur'ãn constantly condemns these interreligious and intrareligious disputes. It attributes them to some kind of malice. They quarrel among themselves because they want to fight each other. Otherwise, if you look into the matter, there is not much to fight about there. The differences of view and interpretation are there, but there is no ground for fighting. And that is why the Qur'ãn laments the intra-Christian differences, for example, and the intra-Jewish differences; and from that it infers that other religions must be the same — that these differences are not always well-meant. It therefore asks mankind to come together, to come together on some kind of a platform, some kind of a formula, where all can be right. It therefore propounded to the "People of the Book" — the Jews and Christians — the invitation:

> A People of the Scripture!
> Come to an agreement between us and you:
> that we shall worship none but God,
> and that we shall ascribe no partner unto Him,
> and that none of us shall take others beside God (3:64).

There is little doubt that the Prophet (pbuh) wanted, alongside of spreading the Qur'anic message, that people should come together in the truth.

This anxiety is so great in the Qur'ãn that the Qur'ãn sometimes says to the Prophet, Why are you so worried? — you are a preacher, you go on preaching. You are not a "warder" over them (4:80; 6:107; 42:48). Leave it to God, as to who accepts and who does not accept; "Let not your soul expire in sighings for them," (35:8) the Qur'ãn says to the Prophet. It's not up to you to force dead men in their graves to listen. God may do that, you can't do that. Your anxiety is understandable, but leave it to God. The Qur'ãn is strewn throughout with such verses (3:176; 7:200; 9:128; 15:97; 18:6). So the anxiety of the Prophet to somehow religiously unify humanity is absolutely obvious. As I said, it's not the case that the Qur'ãn does not allow differences of opinion. In fact, in some way, the Qur'ãn believes that the differences of opinion will go beyond this world, and that they will finally be settled on the Day of Judgement. This notion appears in several verses of the Qur'ãn, the notion that God, on that day, will settle those disputes, those quarrels, those differences of opinion that we have now. However, there must be found, between the absolute alienation, spiritual alienation, of man from man and the total unity of man, there must be found at least a workable, a feasible unity, so that the human race can be called one species, because all human beings are descendants from one spirit, from one source. Of this, the Qur'ãn is absolutely sure — that the roots of all human beings go back to one origin. And that, therefore, humankind must come together, somehow, by mutual understanding, by mutual discussion, which will be the opposite of malice through which they keep on fighting. They might come to a workable world, even if it be not the ideal world, but it should be a workable world.

Well, there are many aspects of the matter of revelation, that is, the content of the Qur'ān. As I said, there is the whole fabric of life there, but I think for this morning, I have probably emphasized certain very basic issues that are directly relevant, starkly relevant to us, the humankind, the human race. Perchance we cannot forget our differences, but we can bring our differences and discuss them in a way and in a spirit that is more constructive than we have been doing in the past.

Thank you very much.

Note: References to the Qur'ān are from The Meaning of the Glorious Koran, Tr. Mohammad Marmadulce Piekthall, New York: The New American Library, n.d.

III

The Qur'an and the Descendants of Korah

BY ERNEST HAMILTON

"Corruption does appear on the land and sea because of what the hands of humankind have done" (30:41)[1], the Qur'an declares. "Lo! humankind is in a state of loss" (103:2), because, being "an ingrate unto its Lord" (100:6), humankind "has not done what He commanded it" (80:23). "Lo!" God says, "We offered the trust unto the heavens and the earth and the hills, but they shrank from bearing it and were afraid of it. And humankind assumed it. Lo! it has proved unjust and very ignorant" (33:72).

Human beings have corrupted the earth through injustice, the Qur'an contends, because most of them follow their own desires. When desires dominate one's self, the Qur'an says, they distort one's perception of the self and of all that to which it relates. In the process one's whole mode of existence becomes egocentric, and one becomes obsessed with the desire for material self-gratification. This obsession with material self-gratification so deludes one that one is unable to act justly towards one's fellow beings and the earth.

Such, briefly stated, is the Qur'anic diagnosis of the ills of humankind in general, which, from the Qur'anic perspective, is equally applicable to the adherents of various theistic religions. What follows, then, is an exploration of the Qur'anic view of the human condition and of the reasons for the failure of most of the believers[2] in God to do good for their fellow creatures.

The Qur'an charges that most theists are in fact "disbelievers" (10:101), "ingrates" (5:67), and "idolaters" (4:51). Such believers, the Qur'an says, contribute to evil and suffering in this world because they fail to engage in *dhikr* —

the constant remembrance of the good God has done for human beings. In the absence of dhikr, their desires and fancies dominate their selves. When dhikr is not the guiding, supporting, and motivating force in the believers' lives, they forget themselves, that is, they forget their true identity and their purpose of existence. Their view of themselves changes when they become oblivious of the notion that they are not autonomous and all-powerful, but interdependent beings of limited power. They forget that they are to live and act in this world as God's vicegerents (2:30; 6:165)[3], and, as such, they are to believe and act in goodness by continually striving for the protection (*taqwa*) and improvement (*islah*) of their fellow beings and themselves.

The Qur'an wishes the believers to relate to their fellow human beings mainly[4] in the context of goodness, compassion, and mercy. It is therefore imperative that the believers remember constantly how God relates to human beings. God, the Qur'an repeatedly reminds the believers, is "the best of the merciful" (23:109, 118); "God has prescribed for Himself mercy" in relation to his creatures (6:12, 54); His "mercy embraces all things" (7:156; 40:7). To underscore the point that God is above all else a God of compassion and mercy[5], each Surah of the Qur'an begins with the invocation "In the name of God, the Compassionate, the Merciful."[6] Further, the Qur'an says that God "ordained" between men and women "love and mercy" (30:21), and in the hearts of people "tenderness and mercy" (57:27). Therefore, "God loves the doers of good" (5:13), and is with them (29:69), and with those who "avert evil with good" (13:22; 28:54, also 41:34), "help one another unto kindness and warding off evil" (5:2), and "exhort one another to patience" and to "mercy" (90:17). God is the ultimate symbol of goodness and compassion. To remember God, therefore, is to remember what true mercy and compassion are; and to remember God's goodness to oneself is to remember to be kind to one's fellow beings.

Further, the Qur'an holds that the believers can attain the knowledge of true goodness only by reflecting on God's goodness and compassion. God's benevolence towards human beings serves as a model and a pattern for them to follow in their conduct with each other. Sura 93, for instance, shows how dhikr reveals guidance to those who engage in it. The Prophet Muhammad is told that 1) God had given him shelter in his orphanhood; *therefore*, he must not oppress the orphan (93:9) but protect him; 2) God had enriched him when he was destitute; *therefore*, he must not drive away the begger (93:10), but enrich him; and 3) God had guided him when he was astray; *therefore*, he must guide those who are astray by declaring to them God's mercies (93:11). The Prophet's remembrance of God's goodness thus reminds him of his true identity — that he is a recipient of God's favors, not a self-sufficient being; he must, therefore, act in goodness toward his fellow creatures as an expression of his sincere gratitude to God for His favors to him. It also revealed to him the nature of true goodness, so that he may do good for his fellow beings in the way God has been good to him. The knowledge of God's goodness to human beings becomes thus the true guide for human conduct, and the remembrance of God's mercies to them (dhikr) their true helper against pride and injustice.

The Believers' Greatest Weakness: Forgetfulness of God's Goodness.

From the Qur'anic perspective, then, whereas the remembrance of God's goodness (dhikr) is the believers' greatest source of strength, their forgetfulness of it is their greatest source of weakness. When the believers are oblivious of the good God has done for them, they forget not only that, as vicegerents of God, they are to act in goodness, but also what true goodness is. When they lose sight of true goodness, they cease to practice true goodness — even though they persist in believing that they are truly doing good (2:11). Once that happens, they commit acts of injustice against the earth, society, and themselves. They forget God's mercies to them, the Qur'an says, at their own peril.

The Qur'anic story of Adam and his mate shows, for instance, how much is at stake when God's benevolence is forgotten. Their obliviousness of God's compassion gives us a clue regarding the manner in which the absence of dhikr leads a believer to be unjust to others and to his/her own self.[8]

"And, verily We made a covenant of old with Adam," God says, "but he forgot, and We found no constancy in him" (20:115). But what was it that he "forgot"? Obviously, Adam did not forget either that God is one or that He exists; Adam and his mate were living in the very presence of God. What Adam forgot was God's mercies to him and his mate. He did not hold on with resoluteness and firmness to the remembrance of God's mercies so that he and his mate would be protected from harm (2:63; 3:103). In failing to remember God, he forgot how good God had been to him and his mate. He forgot that God had 1) made provisions for their physical safety: "It is yours (guaranteed) not to hunger therein nor to go naked/ Nor to thirst, nor to be exposed to the sun" (20:118-119); 2) warned them against both external evil, "O Adam! This (Satan) is an enemy unto you and unto your mate, so let him not drive you both out of the Garden so that you come to toil" (20:117), and internal evil, "O Adam! Dwell you and your mate in the Garden and eat from whence you will, but come not near this tree lest you both be of the unjust" (7:19); 3) taught them knowledge (2:31); and 4) honored (17:62, 70) them by making them His vicegerents on earth (2:30). Adam and his mate forgot God's goodness, and, in forgetting it, they lost sight of true goodness.

Once Adam and his mate became attracted to the idea of attaining "immortality" (20:120) and "enduring power" (20:120), and were deceived (*ghurur*, 7:22) into thinking that it was possible for them to attain their desire, their desire prompted them to act to attain their goal. In the "darkness" (24:40) created by their desire they forgot God's warning against Satan: "Lo! Satan is an open enemy to you" (7:22) and His command: "Come not near this tree lest you become unjust (*zalim*)" (2:35). Consequently, they reached out and attempted the act of injustice (*zulm*) against others, that is, of taking that which was forbidden them and that to which they had no right (7:22). In so doing, they also committed injustice against themselves through self-deception. They forgot their limited power and the role God had assigned to human beings. Consequently, they deceived themselves into thinking that as human beings it was in their power to attain "immortality" and "enduring power" (20:120), and that their desire to do so was good. The consequence of their delusions regarding their identity and potential as human beings was that they were expelled from Paradise (7:27). Further, they were unjust to themselves in that the element of shame entered their world of sexuality. Adam and his mate began to perceive their sexuality as something to hide, to feel ashamed of — as is symbolized by their attempts to cover their bodies: "And when they tasted the tree their shame was manifest to them and they took to stitching upon themselves leaves of the Garden" (7:22). When Adam and his mate realized what they had done, they said to God, "Our Lord! We have been unjust to our own selves" (7:23). The point is that their acts of injustice — violating God's guidance and engaging in self-deception — were the immediate and inevitable consequences of forgetting God's goodness to them.

"Remember Me and I will remember you" (2:152), God says to the believers and warns them, "Be not you as those who forgot God, therefore he caused them to forget themselves. Such are the corruptors" (59:19). As we have seen in the example of Adam and his mate, the immediate result of their temporary obliviousness of God's mercies to them was that they forgot their own selves in that they forgot their purpose of existence and their human limitations. They misperceived their own nature and place in creation, and as a result, they misperceived the nature of Satan, of God, and of existence. Consequently, they committed injustice not only against others but also against themselves.

Further, the story of Satan's disobedience and Adam's forgetfulness makes the point that neither the actual presence of God nor the belief in His oneness (*tawhid*) nor the knowledge of His goodness is in itself effective in guiding behavior.[9] Both Satan (7:11) and Adam acted (7:22) in the very presence of God as if God was not really present. God was to both Adam and Satan conceptually and visually present but not mentally. That is, when Satan and Adam made a decision to act, God was not their "partner" (7:30) in their decision making. The memory of God's mercies was pushed back in Adam's consciousness and was replaced by the desire of immortality and enduring power. They acted in the presence of God as if, for them, to all practical purposes, God did not exist. To remember that God exists and that God is one, thus, is not truly to remember God; but to remember God to the extent that remembrance of God's goodness motivates one to do good for one's fellow beings is truly to remember God; it is truly to be in the state of dhikr.

Kinds of Forgetfulness

Forgetfulness of God's benevolence towards human beings, then, from the Qur'anic perspective, is the chief cause of evil and suffering. The Qur'an uses two different words to express such forgetfulness: *nasiya*, to forget, and *ghafla*, to be heedless or unmindful of something. Forgetfulness of God's goodness is a phenomenon which manifests itself in a variety of ways, from a simple loss of memory to deliberate acts of forgetfulness and unmindfulness. And all believers, of all ranks and stations, prophets and ordinary people, are subject to it.[10]

A. *Nasiya.* The earliest reference in the Qur'an to human forgetfulness concerns the Prophet Muhammad when God says to him: "We shall cause you to read, so that you forget (nasiya) not, except what God wills" (87:6-7). Here, in an early Meccan Sura, the word nasiya is employed to indicate a temporary inability to recall or an unintentional failure to remember something.

The word nasiya is employed in the Qur'an with various meanings, such as inadvertently forgetting to do something: "Our Lord! Take us not to task if we forget or make a mistake" (2:286), or when Moses and his servant forgot to bring the fish along with them (18:71). Another kind of forgetting is where one does something against one's intention because of some inner compulsion, as in the case of Moses' constant and irritable questioning of his companion (18:73). Other instances are forgetting to see the connection between two things — "And with those who say: 'Lo! We are Christians,' We made a covenant, but they forgot a part of that whereof they were admonished" (5:14; 2:44); ceasing to be concerned about something due to the passage of time (25:18); forgetting something which is perceived as of no immediate concern, such as the Judgment Day (7:51); forgetting something because the need to remember it has passed (6:41; 39:8); forgetting something because of preoccupation with other things (59:19); and forgetting something because it is not considered important to remember (9:67).

B. *Ghafla.* If nasiya denotes a failing of memory, however temporary and for whatever reason, then, ghafla, another word used in the Qur'an to indicate human forgetfulness, denotes a lack of awareness or consciousness of something, however that lack may have come about and for whatever reason it may have continued. And, as we shall presently see, the term ghafla is employed in the Qur'an to indicate not only a plain unawareness of something, but also of deliberately paying no heed to it.

The term ghafla is not employed in the Qur'an until the second period of the Meccan Suras, and it is first mentioned in connection with the Judgment Day, where it is said to an evildoer on the Judgment Day, "You were in heedlessness (*fi ghaflatin*) of this (day)" (50:22). That is, he was warned (50:28) of the coming of the Judgment Day but he disbelieved it (50:24) and willfully paid no heed to it. He represents those who know but willfully ignore and pay no heed to what they know (7:136).

In addition, one may be in the state of ghafla when one knows something but can't pay attention to it because one is distracted by something else (4:102; 12:13); when one is too busy to notice what happened (28:15); when one knows but acts indiscreetly (24:23); when one knows but is not really concerned about the consequences of ignoring it (21:1; 21:97); when one does something wrong because one is not aware of the right thing to do (6:131, 156; 7:172); when one is simply unaware of something taking place (10:29; 46:5); and when one does not make an effort to notice something happening (10:92).

Factors Contributing to Human Forgetfulness.

Further, the Qur'an shows that the nature of existence, that is, the reality of human nature, the process of living in this world, the attractions of the life of this world, and the nature of evil, is such that it tends to make people forget God's goodness and compassion.

A. *Some Human Characteristics*. With regard to the characteristics that make human beings forgetful of God's goodness, the Qur'an says that 1) human beings were created "in affliction (*fi kabadin*, literally, the affliction caused by an injury to the liver)" (90:4); 2) they were "created of haste" (21:37); 3) they are forgetful (20:115); 4) they are inconstant (20:115) and fretful ("surely man was created fretful," 70:19), so that, God says about human beings,

> If We cause man to taste some mercy from Us and afterwards withdraw it from him, lo! he is despairing, thankless. And if We cause him to taste grace after some misfortune that had befallen him, he says: The ills have gone from me. Lo! he is exultant, boastful (11:9-10).

And,

> as for man, whenever His Lord tries him by honoring him, he says; My Lord honors me. But whenever he tries him by straightening his means of life, he says: My Lord despises me" (89:15-16).

Lastly, although human beings are created "of the best stature" (95:4), they are created "weak" (4:28).

Thus, the reality of human nature, according to the Qur'an, is that human beings were created hasty, inconstant, forgetful, in affliction, and weak; and, as such, if the believers do not strive continually to remember God's goodness to them, then like Adam and his mate, they will not be strong enough to resist the temptations the world presents to them.

B. *Some Characteristics of This World.*

1. *The Joys of Life*. "The life of the world," the Qur'an says, "beguiles" those who fail to remember God's goodness (6:70; 130), even though "this present life is but illusory enjoyment" (3:185). The life of the world with its "adornments" (11:15) — family, material prosperity, pleasures, and comforts — and those who possess them, are powerful and constant sources of distraction (24:37) for human beings, even for prophets (see Soloman, 38:32; Muhammad, 18:29). "Made to seem fair," the Qur'an says, "is the life of the world for those who disbelieve" (2:212). They find contentment (9:38) in it, and rejoice (13:26) in it, so that they desire (11:15) it, prefer it (87:16), and love (76:27) it. People "prefer the present life" (87:16) because

> beautified for the people is love of the joys from women and offspring, and stored up heaps of gold and silver, and horses branded, and cattle and land. That is comfort of the life of the world (3:14).

"Merchandise" and "sale" (24:37), "spouses" (64:14), and "wealth and children" distract them "from the remembrance of God" (63:9). They "eat and enjoy life and let hope beguile them" (15:3). In failing to remember God's goodness, people fail to see that the "life of the world is but comfort of illusion" (57:20). It is "a pastime and a sport" (6:32; 29:64), a "brief comfort" (13:26), and "that which hastens away" (17:18). "Know," the Qur'an says,

> that the life of the world is only play, and idle talk and pageantry, and boasting among you and rivalry in respect of wealth and children; as the likeness of vegetation after rain, whereof the growth is pleasing to the husbandman, but afterwards it dries up and you see it turning yellow, then it becomes straw (57:20; also 18:45).

This world's comforts are neither permanent nor an end in themselves. "Lo! We have placed in the earth all that is in the earth as an ornament thereof," God says, "that We may try them: which of them is best of conduct" (18:7), for "wealth and sons are an ornament of life of the world, but the deeds that set things right — the things which endure — are better" (18:46).

2. *The Effects of Prosperity and Success*. Another misguiding factor (6:70) in life is the envy which the success of many people in attaining wealth, comforts, and power arouses in others. For example, Korah

> went forth unto his people in his pomp. Those who were desirous of the life of the world said: Ah, would that unto us had been given the like of what has been given to Korah! Lo! he is a lord of rare good fortune (28:79).

Another example is that of Pharaoh, whose wealth Moses asked God to destroy, because "You have given Pharaoh and his chiefs splendor and riches in the life of the world. Our Lord! that they may lead men astray from Your way" (10:88). Also, in Sura 33:67, we find some of the ingrates complaining on the Judgment Day to God, "Our Lord! Lo! we obeyed our princes and our great ones, and they led us astray from the Way" (33:67).

3. *The Effect of the Passage of Time.* The Qur'an also notes the effect of time on human beings and shows that the mere passage of time obliterates the remembrance of God's goodness so that the believers are left without any guidance. On the Judgment Day, when God will ask who misled a certain group of people, He will be told, "You did give them and their fathers enjoyment of days, until they forgot the remembrance and became lost folk" (25:18). About another group who were punished for turning away from His remembrance due to passage of time, God says, "But We gave these and their fathers enjoyment of days until life grew long for them" (21:44, see also 20:86-87; 28:45).

This is not to say that the Qur'an sees all evil and suffering in the world solely as a consequence of human forgetfulness. It does not. In fact, it is fully aware of the difficulties under which human beings live and function. "Man was created in affliction," the Qur'an acknowledges, and perhaps a most potent element in that affliction is the kind of evil which is independent of human beings and is of cosmic proportions. It is the kind of evil which so surrounds humankind that they have no escape from it, and there is an admission in the Qur'an that even the best of human beings cannot escape it.

C. *The Nature of Evil.*

1. *Natural Evil.* There are a few verses in the Qur'an which deal with the evil of things that God has created, both sentient and insentient. The Qur'an states that all manifestations of creation have both benign and evil aspects, as we see in the following verses: "Say, I seek refuge in the Lord of the Daybreak/From the evil (*sharr*) of what He created/And from the evil of the darkening when it comes on" (113:1-3), and, "By a self (*nafs*) and that which formed it and inspired it to disintegration (*fujur*, literally, a breaking up) and to warding off evil (*taqwa*) (91:7-8).

2. *Cosmic Evil.* One also gets the impression that there is evil within the creation itself; and that it is a force that has always been discordant, perhaps even before the creation of humankind. In the Qur'anic story of humankind's creation, for instance, we see this discordant force personified as Iblis, or Satan. The figure of Satan represents the view that there is more to evil than just human error and willful wrongdoing. Thus Satan represents evil that is beyond human evil and beyond human comprehension. When God created Adam and brought him before the heavenly beings, He asked the heavenly beings to prostrate themselves before Adam. "And they fell prostrate," the Qur'an says, "all save Iblis (Satan), who was not of those who prostrate(d?)" (7:11). The phrase "*lam yakun min al-sajidin*" may be translated correctly either as "not of those who prostrated" or "not of those who prostrate," that is, not of those who are in the habit of prostrating. In the former case it would mean that the disobedience of Satan began after the creation of human beings.

Whatever the case, Satan's pride and the consequent act of disobedience manifested themselves certainly after Adam's creation and are the result of it. Also, Satan was not the only one among the heavenly beings who was displeased by the appearance of human beings. When God announces His intention to place Adam as His vicegerent on the earth the angels protested, saying, "will you place someone who will work corruption and shed blood?" (2:30). The story seems to imply that, whether or not there was disharmony in the universe before the appearance of human beings, there was certainly disharmony after their creation. The appearance of human beings created a strong negative reaction in the forces of the universe, ranging from protests to outright rebellion.

In any case, it is evident from the story that the evil which Satan represents is not of humankind's making. Satan exhibited his evil of pride (2:34) and disobedience (2:34) even before human beings were aware or conscious of such evils. In fact, the story shows that human evil manifested itself only in response to the evil that existed prior to it. Adam and his mate's wrong thoughts (desiring to be immortal and to possess enduring power) and wrong action (using the unjust means to attain their desire) follow in time Satan's wrongs of pride and disobedience. Satan is labelled as the "degraded one" (7:13) even before man commited injustice against himself (2:35).

The Qur'anic story of creation, then, indicates that while many other forces would be conducive to human growth (e.g., "Unto God makes prostration whatsoever is in the heavens and watsoever is in the earth," 22:17; and "living creatures, and the angels, and they are not proud," 16:49), at least one force would be inimical to it. Further, it is clear that humankind too, like the creation before it, is to be subject to the workings of this discordant force. God not only fails to refute Satan's charge against Him (e.g., "you have sent (or caused), me to go astray/perverted," 7:1-6), but also grants Satan's request to allow him to deceive humankind ("Reprieve me till the day when they are raised," 7:14; "I verily shall adorn the path of error for them in the earth, and shall beguile them every one," 15:39). In fact, God tells Satan to do his worst to tempt humankind: "And excite any of them, whom you can with your voice, and urge your horse and foot against them, and be a partner in their wealth and children, and promise them" (17:64). Human beings are not to be immune from the attacks of evil as long as they exist. God decided neither to destroy nor to check this force that was to adversely affect humankind, but rather to expressly give it "reprieve" (7:15), that is, let it operate unhindered in the universe to play its role in the drama of human existence. Some evil, whether primordial or not, is allowed to continue and to adversely affect creation, including humankind, until the Judgment Day. Thus not all evil proceeds from human beings. And, as has been shown, the Qur'an clearly acknowledges it. It leaves the mystery of the origin of evil intact, presumably and because it is concerned chiefly with evil and suffering caused by human beings.

Whatever the origin of cosmic evil, the Qur'an is very clear about its significance for the believers. The Qur'an warns that Satan is a "manifest foe" (2:168) of humankind. He "seeks only to cast" among them "enmity and hatred" (5:91), "promises poverty," and "bids unto indecency" (2:268), and inspires "tinsel speech" to "delude" (6:112). Satan introduced feelings of shame into human sexuality (7:20). He tempts (7:27), perverts (7:175), and incites (7:200). He interferes in the process of revelation (22:52). He encourages what is "disreputable" (24:21), afflicts people with weariness and torment (38:41), suggests evil (23:97), and turns them aside from the way of God (29:38; 43:62).

Satan gains mastery over the believers (58:19), the Qur'an says, through making them forget God (5:91). He makes people forget God by employing deceptive means (4:120). First, he stirs up desire in them (4:119) by making things of this world appear beautiful to them (15:39). Then, he makes false promises (4:120) to deceive them into thinking that, 1) what they desire can be attained easily and instantly (7:20-22), and 2) the means they emloy to fulfill their desire are "good" (38:8). Further, the Qur'an warns the believers: "Satan sees you, he and his tribe, from whence you see him not" (7:27), meaning, perhaps, that Satan and his ways are beyond human comprehension.

The Qur'an sees Satan as an aggressive and untiring foe who is always on the offensive against humankind, as Satan himself declares to God:

Now because you have sent me astray,
verily I shall lurk in ambush for them on thy right path,
then I shall come upon them from before them, and
from their right hands, and
from their left hands, and
you will not find most of them showing gratitude (7:16-17).

It is important to note, however, that Satan is presented in the Qur'an as an aggressive agent only in terms of persuasion through constant suggestions and whisperings (114:4-6) to human beings, never in terms of the actual use of force. Satan is never presented as employing force to coerce human beings into doing injustice. That remains the prerogative of human beings only.

These verses about Satan indicate the kind of evil the believers have to deal with. Thus, the character of Satan, in the drama of humankind's creation, may be understood as a personification of evil with the following characteristics: 1) it is a discordant force in the cosmos (7:12); 2) it existed before the evil created by human beings (7:11); 3) it is distinct and independent of the evil created by humankind; 4) it will continue to exist as long as humankind continues to exist (7:14); 5) unlike other forces in the universe, it will adversely affect and influence human behavior (7:11); 6) it cannot be overcome and destroyed by human beings (7:14); 7) humankind is unable to comprehend it (7:27); 8) it is a hostile and malignant power (2:36); and 9) it is an unmitigatedly aggressive force (7:16-17).[11]

Such, according to the Qur'an, is the real nature of human beings and the world in which they live. Human weakness, inconstancy, haste, forgetfulness, the attraction of the joys of life, the effects of success, the effects of the passage of time, the evil aspect of created things, and the onslaughts of an aggressive cosmic evil indeed provide a formidable array of forces for the believer to face. Only a constant remembrance of God's goodness and compassion, the Qur'an insists, can save them from forgetting the truth about themselves and the world. The believer exists, the Qur'an say, as one on the "brink of an abyss of fire" (3:103) or on the "brink of a crumbling, overhanging precipice" above the "fire of hell" (9:109). Only by holding on fast and clinging to the "cable" (3:103) of the remembrance of God's goodness can the believers be safe from falling "into the fire of hell" (9:109).

Consequences of Forgetfulness

Zulm (Injustice). When the believers forget God's goodness and compassion, then, the Qur'an insists, whatever they perceive, whatever they think, and whatever they do is bound to be unjust (*zulm*).

The term zulm refers to the act of "putting something in the wrong place"; it is "to do injustice in the sense of going beyond one's own bounds and doing what one has no right to."[12] "To associate others with God," the Qur'an says, "is a great injustice" (31:13). In committing the injustice of making desire equal to God, for example one commits an act of injustice against desire in that one places it where it does not belong, and thus distorts the notion and function of human desire; one does injustice to the notion of God by putting God on the same level with human desire where God does not belong, and thus distorts the notion and role of God; and one commits injustice against one's self by putting one's self in the wrong place with regard to one's desire and to God, and thus distorts the notion and role of the self. Moreover, if one is in a position of influence, then one's doing so might also misguide others.

The act of "putting" something "in the wrong place," such as desire, is, thus, to attempt to violate its "bounds," that is, to conceptually distort its nature and function. Such an attempt also violates one's own bounds, for one has no right to try to distort the nature and function of things as they are. Zulm is, therefore, violation of the rights not only of others but also of one's own self.

Further, as the Qur'an shows, zulm or injustice may be perpetrated either through the use of force or through the use of guile. When the egocentric self cannot attain fulfillment of its desire by "force" (26:130), it attempts to attain it through "deception" (35:40). Deception and force, then, are the two basic means through which the unjust person may attain self-gratification. When the believers do not remember the good God has done for them, the Qur'an holds, they invariably turn to the use of deception and force as a means to attain self-gratification. "The unjust promise one another only to deceive," (35:40; 4:120), the Qur'an notes. The unjust lure by false promises those whom they cannot coerce by force. Satan promised Adam and his mate "immortality" and "enduring power" only to deceive them into doing injustice against themselves (20:115-121). The Qur'an offers an example of a believer who would deceive even God through false promises to attain his selfish ends:

> ...of them is he who made a covenant with God: if He gave us of His bounty we will give alms and become of those who set things right. Yet when He gave them of His bounty, they become niggardly with it and turn away averse (9:75-76).

The Workings of Forgetfulness

In order to understand how the obliviousness to God's goodness leads both to forgetfulness of the self and, consequently, to injustice, we must look into the imagery the Qur'an employs regarding the life of the believer. It views the believer's life as a journey from God to God (10:34): the believer starts his journey, at birth, from God and ends it, at death, before God. Believers may travel either on the "straight path" (1:6) or on the "path of error" (7:146). If they stay on the straight path till the end of their journey, they receive the fairest "resort" and "homecoming" (3:14), or Paradise. They are the "prosperers" (30:38). If they follow the "path of error," they receive an "ill resort" and an "evil homecoming" (38:55), 8:16), or Hell. They are the "losers" (7:178).[11] The straight path is a "steep uphill path" (90:12) that runs through the regions of darkness and can be seen only with the help of dhikr; for dhikr serves as a light (39:22) and reveals the straight path that is otherwise obscured in the darkness.

With dhikr as the light to show them the Way, the believers progress in their journey toward God by competing with each other, as in a race, in doing good for their fellow beings (2:148). To those who continually "strive" (5:35) in the race to do good for their fellow beings, God and His angels serve as supporters (41:30; 66:4) and protecting friends (4:123) to help overcome the distractions and hardships on the way to their destination (2:62; 3:103; 22:38). The believers can see the straight path and remain on it, however, only as long as they continue to engage in dhikr. The moment they forget God's goodness, the light of dhikr is obscured by their forgetfulness, and they deviate from (29:38) or move off (6:87) the straight path and are suddenly overwhelmed by darkness (2:257). In the darkness, they take the "path of error," where Satan and his minions become their companions (4:119; 43:36) and exhort them to race with each other in sin and transgression (5:62) and debarring others from the straight path (43:62). If the believers do not strive to return to the straight path through dhikr, but continue to travel in darkness, any path they take will eventually lead them to the gates of Hell (16:29).

The State of Being Lost.

It is in this context that the Qur'an uses the word *dalla*, to go astray, in order to indicate the believer's first misstep, in his life-journey, toward injustice. Those believers who forget God's mercies go "astray" (17:48) in the sense that their self-perception changes, and with that their motivation for and manner of dealing with their fellow beings. They view themselves as "masters of the earth" (10:24) and believe that all beings and things exist only to serve them. They forget that they are God's "vicegerents" (6:165; 35:39) who are given the "trust" (*amanah*, 33:72) to do good for their fellow creatures and the earth. This moment of change in one's self-perception is variously described in the Qur'an, for instance, as the moment when "Satan caused them (Adam and his mate) to slip therefrom" (*azalla*, to cause someone to slip or slide back, 2:36), or when Adam "erred" (*ghawa*, to err, 20:121), or "went astray" (*dalla*, to lose way, to go astray, 20:123; *dalal*, the state of being lost).

In Arabic the word dalla originally meant losing one's way while traveling in the desert.[14] Perhaps the earliest use of the term in the Qur'an occurs in connection with the Prophet himself, where he is reminded that he had erred or gone astray (*dallan*) once himself — a reference to his state of uncertainty regarding the nature of his relationship with God — until God guided him (93:7).

Other early uses of the term dalal relate to the opponents of the Prophet, who charged that the Prophet was "mad" (68:2) and "demented" (68:6). In response the Qur'an says to the Prophet, "Your Lord knows best who strays (dalla) from His way and He knows who are rightly guided" (68:7), implying that it is certainly not Muhammad who has gone wrong. The term dalal is also used to indicate how God "sends astray," that is, makes futile, the actions of those who are over-confident in their power (105:2) or in their prosperity

(68:10-33), and who thereby show their ingratitude (*kufr*) to God. Further, by using the word dalal, the Qur'an implies two things: 1) to forget God is to necessarily go off the right path, and 2) to go off the right path is to necessarily be lost. When the believers forget God's goodness they cannot help but proceed in the wrong direction and act in the wrong manner. Thus those believers who are forgetful of God's mercies are in the state of dalal — of having lost their way. To be without dhikr, then, is to be in the state of dalal.

The Regions of Darkness.

When the believers turn around (29:38) and move off the "straight" path (6:87), they go astray and find themselves lost in "darkness" (2:17), for the straight path is surrounded by the regions of darkness.

The Qur'an uses the imagery of light and darkness and sight and blindness to illustrate the constrast between those who live in the world of dhikr, the world created by the believers' remembrance of God's goodness, and those who live in the world of *zulumat*, the world created by their forgetfulness of God's mercies. Those who remember God constantly are those who can see their way in this world because the remembrance of God's goodness serves as a light to show them the way of goodness; they are the "seers" (40:58). Those who forget God cannot see because they have not the light that accompanies the remembrance of God's compassion to show them the way of true goodness in this world; they are the "blind" (40:58). "Those whose hearts are hardened against the remembrance of God," the Qur'an says, are not like the one "who follows a light from his Lord" (39:22); rather

> their likeness is as the likeness of one who kindles fire, and when it sheds its light around him God takes away their light and leaves them in darkness, where they cannot see. Deaf, dumb, and blind, and they return not (2:17-20).

Or they are like one enshrouded in

> darkness on a vast, abysmal sea. There covers him a wave, above which is a wave, above which is a cloud. Layer upon layer of darkness. When he holds out his hand he scarce can see it (24:40).

Thus, "they are all astray and cannot find a way" (17:48). Forgetfulness of God's mercies, whether it issues from human weaknesses or from a deliberate disregard of God's guidance, leads to the same consequence: zulumat, the condition in which the believers think and behave like those who have lost their way and are traveling in "utter darkness" (6:122).

To be without the remembrance of God's compassion, in other words, is to be in ignorance regarding the true nature of the self, goodness, and this world. It is to become mentally blind to true goodness just as surely as to lose one's eyesight is to become physically blind to the things in this world. Dhikr serves as one's eyes, the Qur'an says, for without dhikr one is like the blind, living and moving in utter darkness. Therefore, God says in the Qur'an,

> Whoso follows My guidance, he will not go astray nor become miserable. But he who turns away from remembrance of Me, his will be a narrow life, and I shall bring him blind to the assembly of the Day of Resurrection. He will say: My Lord! wherefore have you raised me here blind, though I used to see clearly? He (God) will say: Thus (it is). Our signs came unto you, but you did forget them. In like manner you are forgotten this Day (20:124-126).

"Whoso blinds himself to the remembrance of the All-Merciful" (43:36) is blind to the good of others and, therefore, to his own good — even though he thinks he sees "clearly" and is "acting uprightly" (2:11). Thus deluded, his life will be made "narrow" (20:124) by fear and sorrow (2:62). And, "whoso is blind here (in this world), " God warns, "will be blind in the Hereafter" (17:72).

The World of Delusions.

Once the believers enter the regions of darkness (zulumat), they take the "path of error" (7:146), which leads to the world of delusions (*gharur*, 67:20). The world of delusions is created by those believers who, for whatever reason, are bereft of the remembrance of God's mercies to them. The "rule of conduct" (17:84) of the denizens of this world is injustice, and desire is their god. The pathways of injustice are beautified by Satan (15:39), the "Deluder" (31:33), so that most things appear to be what they are not: 1) the evil appears to be good and the good evil (27:4); 2) the impossible appears possible and the possible impossible (20:120); 3) the certain appears doubtful and the doubtful certain (18:34-36); and 4) the transient appears permanent and the permanent transient (104:2-3). The world of delusions (gharur) is, thus, a world of falsehood (*batil*), not truth (*haqq*) (2:42). Living in this world, the believers are ever deceived. "As for those who are ungrateful," the Qur'an says, "their patrons are false gods. They bring them out of light into darkness" (2:257). When the believers make desire their god, it makes them "slide back" from the light of truth into the darkness of delusions. "The ungrateful" exist, the Qur'an says, "in nothing but delusion" (67:20). To live in the regions of darkness is to operate on the basis of delusions.

Delusions About the Self. "Be not you as those who forgot God, therefore He caused them to forget their selves" (59:19), the Qur'an warns the believers; for one of the ways a believer commits injustice against himself when he goes astray and lives in the world of delusions is to misperceive his own self.

A. *Self-Sufficiency.* When, in his state of ignorance, a believer loses the memory of knowleedge of any being higher than his own self, his self becomes the sole focus of his attention. In the darkness of his forgetfulness of God, only his self shines. When a believer's self is thus magnified, he "thinks himself independent (*istaghna*)" (96:7), the Qur'an says, because he forgets the ways in which God has been good to him.

The verb istaghna is derived from the root *GH N Y*, meaning to be rich or wealthy. From this root the word *ghaniyy* is formed and applied to God to indicate that God is so rich that He can stand alone. He does not need anything or anyone. He is thus an absolutely autonomous, independent, and self-sufficient being.

The believer who is oblivious of God's mercies wishes to be independent like God. He becomes like one "who has gathered wealth and arranged it. He thinks that his wealth will render him immortal" (104:2-3). A very early description of such a person is found in Sura 96:

> But verily man is insolent (tagha), because he thinks himself self-sufficient (istaghna, 96:6-7).
> Have you seen if he follows the guidance (of God)? (96:11).
> Have you seen if he denies and turns away?
> Does he not know that God sees? (96:13-14).

B. *Insolence*. This illusion of istaghna (self-sufficiency) leads the believer to a state of mind which the Qur'an calls *tughyan* (96:6), or insolence. The word *tagha* is used in the Qur'an to mean to be insolent, to be overbold; it originally referred to the phenomenon of a river swelling and overflowing its banks.[15] It is meant to convey the sense of a power gone out of control.

In other words, when the believers become oblivious of God's mercies, they see themselves as all-sufficient and autonomous beings — full of unbounded self-confidence. This feeling, then, makes them swollen with self-conceit; they become insolent (tagha). They are like one who, the Qur'an says, thinks that "none has power over him," and he boasts" "I have destroyed vast wealth." He thinks that "none beholds him" (90:5-7).

Desire as God.

Next, being in this state of insolence, the believers let their desires (*ahwa'*) and fancies (*amani*) guide them in their thoughts and actions. He "whose heart" is "heedless of Our remembrance," God says, "follows his own desire" (18:29). Those believers who have forgotten God's compassion, even temporarily, are then led solely by their desires.

Consequences of Being Led by Desire.

"Have you seen," the Qur'an asks the Prophet Muhammad, "him who has taken his own desire (ahwa') as his god (*ilah*)?"[16] He goes "astray" (25:42) and his "affair" becomes "all excess" (18:28). When the believer is solely under the domination of desires, then his view of the world and his mode of dealing with his fellow human beings also change.

A. *Subjectivity*. The psychological effect on those who are led by desire is that it distorts their perception; they are unable to see the world, their own selves, and good and evil as they really are. When subjective desires are the only arbiter of reality, they distort the perception of reality to suit their objective ("They follow but a guess and that which they themselves desire," 53:23). This process of subjective perception leads the believers to make gross and tragic error; "Lo! many are led astray by their own desires," the Qur'an says, "through ignorance" (6:119). The Qur'an compares a person who has taken subjective desire as his god to the spider and its web.

> The likeness of those who choose patrons other than God is as the likeness of the spider; it makes for itself a house, and lo! the frailest of all houses is the spider's house, if they but knew (29:41).

In other words, the acts and thoughts out of which the desire-dominated self weaves its world are, like the spider's web, built from its own entrails, from its own subjective desires, which have no basis in truth and reality. Desires, the Qur'an says, produce only an distorted view of whatever one does and thinks and sees.

2. *Rigidity and Narrow-Mindedness.* Because the egocentric believer is governed by subjective desires, the Qur'an says, he becomes narrow-minded and rigid like one with "bosom narrow and contracted as if he were engaged in sheer ascent into the heaven" (96:125). He becomes "niggardly" (17:100), "stubborn," and unresponsive:

> he clings to the earth and follows his own desire. Therefore his likeness is as the likeness of a dog; if you attack him he pants with his tongue out, and if you leave him he pants with his tongue out" (7:176).

When his delusions are challenged he becomes contentious (18:54). He is persistent in his "insolence" (23:75); and he wanders "blindly" (23:75) in his "disdain and aversion" to truth (67:21). His "heart and hearing are sealed," and his sight is "covered" (45:23). The hearts of such believers, the Qur'an says, are protected from any calls, as if in their ears there is a deafness, and between them and the callers there is a veil (41:5). They turn away in their "pride" as if they have not heard (31:7) and "wander away" from the "Way of God" (38:26). So whether they are warned or not it is the same for them, for their are "shackles on their necks, reaching up to the chin, so they hold their heads in the air," and there is "a barrier before them, and a barrier behind them, and they are covered so that they cannot see" (36:8-9). They are all "astray and cannot find a way" (17:48).

3. *Selfishness.* The self that is governed by desire may be understood as the self which exists simply to satisfy its own desires. It is a self that confesses sincere belief in one God (*tawhid*) but loves another god — the god of desire, of self-gratification, of instant satisfaction of the senses, of the desire for power (35:10), prosperity (73:11), and enjoyment (46:20). In the absence of dhikr, the concerns of the self dominate the senses and the self becomes blind, deaf, and hard-hearted to anything other than the promptings (50:16) of desires (6:19) and fancies (57:14). Thus the egocentric self thinks and acts solely in the interest of itself. In doing so, it fails to see the injustice of its actions, because the justification for its actions lies not in the good of others but in the attainment of its own desires. The selfish believer turns to God only to seek help in times of trouble and for material gain:

> When some hurt touches man, he cries unto his Lord, turning unto him (repentant). Then when He grants him a boon from Him, he forgets that which he cried unto Him before, and sets up rivals to God" (39:8; also, 9:75-76).

The same is true of his relationships with his fellow beings: "The unjust," the Qur'an says, "promises one another only to deceive" (35:40). Selfishness is, then, the real motive of such believers' relationship with God and with human beings. Thoughts and actions that are generated by selfishness are perceived by the Qur'an as necessarily unjust. Thus, "those who commit injustice follow their own desires without knowledge" (30:29).

4. *Impulsiveness*. The Qur'an holds that when the believers are guided by desire, they cannot but engage in impulsive actions. As stated earlier, the kind of self the desires command is the self which suffers from the feeling of insolence (tughyan). The self in the state of insolence overflows with self-confidence. Insolence (tagha) is really, then, an unbounded, out of control, sense of automony — of istaghna. The fact that it is "unbounded" indicates that it is not restricted or restrained by anything. Desire wishes not to be stopped or frustrated in attaining satisfaction either by time or by principles. Actions arising out of desire are thus necessarily impulsive actions.

5. *Irresponsibility*.

> And Satan indeed found his calculation true concerning them, for they follow him, all save a group of true believers. And he had no power whatsoever over them, save that We would know him who believes in the Hereafter from him who is in doubt thereof; and your Lord takes not all things (34:20-21).

As the verse clearly shows, those who follow Satan are those who do not believe in the Hereafter, that is, they do not believe in accountability for their actions. The main reason there is a Judgment Day, after all, is to judge the mode of being of each individual and to ask him/her to account for his/her way of existence. Inasmuch as the notion of the Judgment Day stands for the accountability of human actions, the misguided believers' strategy is either to profess an outright denial of it as a supernatural event or try to minimize its import for them. "We know not what the Hour (the Judgment Day) is. We deem it nothing but a conjecture, and we are by no means convinced" (45:32), some of them said to the Prophet. Others granted the possibility of the Judgment Day's coming but sought to mitigate its effect by saying either that they would not be held fully accountable for their ill deeds because they would be forgiven (7:169), or that they would at most be punished mildly (3:24). Underlying the denial of the Judgment Day is their desire not to be hampered by any sense of responsibility for their actions. About them the Qur'an says, "lo! Those who believe not in the Hereafter are indeed deviating from the (right) path" (23:74). Consequently, those who do not think they are responsible for their actions are unconcerned about the unjustice of their actions. The Qur'an says: "Those who believe not in the Hereafter," their works are made "fair-seeming unto them to that they are all astray" (27:4). From the Qur'anic perspective, then, belief in the Judgment Day is the supreme test and the clearest indication of whether or not one accepts responsibility for one's actions.

6. *Materialism.* The Qur'an shows that the focus of subjective desires is this world and what it offers to please the senses. The believers under the domination of desire therefore seek only material pleasures and comforts. They become obsessed with this material world and what it has to offer (18:28). They say, "There is nothing but our life of the world; we die and we live, and nothing destroys us save time" (45:24), and they "rejoice" in the life of the world (13:26). Further, such obsession with this world makes them greedy. The Qur'an says that each human being is created "alone" (74:11), that is, with only that which is necessary for his survival; God has given him "ample means, and sons abiding in his presence, and made everything smooth for him." "Yet," God says, "he desires that I should give him more" (74:11-15). People who are led by their desires are never content with what they have but ever demand more, so that "rivalry with one another in wealth occupies" them until they "come to their graves" (102:1-2). Such people "are very prone to greed" (4:128); they "devour the inheritance with devouring greed," and "love wealth with abounding love" (89:19-20). Driven by greed, they hoard their wealth (92:8). They perceive themselves as "masters" of the earth (10:24) and believe their wealth will render them "immortal" (104:2). On the other hand, when it comes to giving, they are stingy and niggardly (33:19). They "urge not the feeding of the poor" (89:18), and they refuse to share their wealth with the needy. In addition, since they believe that this is the only life they have, they direct all their energies to enrich their material life by seeking "power" (35:10), "prosperity" (73:11), and "enjoyment" (46:20). And, viewing the attainment of power, prosperity, and enjoyment as the sole purpose of life, they judge the value of all thought, human endeavor, and life in terms of material success. In the Qur'anic parable of a proud and humble man, for instance, the proud man believes that his material prosperity must be a sign of God's approval of him. He says to his companion, "I am more than you in wealth and stronger in respect of men," and concludes, "I think not that all this will ever perish: I think not that the Hour will ever come (that is, he will not be held accountable for his deeds), and if indeed I am brought back unto my Lord I surely shall find better than this resort" (18:34-36).

7. *Moral Blindness.* Such materialism of the believers also deceives them into thinking that they are "rightly guided" (6:123). "The good deeds[17] and the evil deeds are not alike." Repel the evil deed with that which is better, then," the Qur'an says, "lo! he, between whom and you there was enmity, (will become) as though he was a bosom friend" (41:34). But those who "blind themselves to the remembrance of the Compassionate" (43:36), the Qur'an warns, have no guidance, and, therefore, they lose the ability to distinguish between good and evil, so that when they do evil "they think they are rightly guided" (43:36-37). They are like one "the evil of whose deeds is made fair-seeming unto him so

that he deems it good" (35:8; also 6:122). They mistake good for evil and evil for good because desire blinds them to the injustice of their actions. Desire produces only selfish acts, and selfish acts cannot contribute to the welfare of anyone.

The Qur'an thus insists on the reflexive nature of human actions; any harm or good done to other is harm or good done to one's own self. "Whoso sets things right (*islah*), it is for his own self, and who so does wrong (*asa*), it is against his own self" (41:46; 45:15). Since every act has consequences, an act done for the good of others contributes to the process of self-purification (91:9), thereby bringing one nearer to God (56:11). An act done for the harm of others contributes to the process of self-corruption (91:10), thereby bringing one closer to self-destruction (80:17). Thus the Qur'an views the well-being or destruction of one's own self as inextricably bound with the well-being or destruction of one's fellow creatures. To think, therefore, that one can benefit through injustice to others is to delude oneself. Consequently, the Qur'an constantly reminds the believers that to commit injustice against others in the hope of attaining good for oneself is in reality to commit injustice against one's own self (4:110), even though the harm done to one's own self in the process is obscured at the time by the feeling of elation at having succeeded in attaining the good one desired (3:188; 40:75).

Therefore, the good for which they toil and struggle, the Qur'an says, is "as a mirage in a desert. The thirsty one supposes it to be water till he comes unto it and finds it nothing" (24:39). Just as a person overcome by thirst is deceived into imagining water where there is no water so is the person led by selfish desire deceived into imagining good where there is no good. Thus, the person who is overcome by desire thinks that his actions are "good" (27:4) when they are not and that he is "rightly guided" (43:36-37) when he is not.

From the Qur'anic perspective, then, the self ruled by desire can neither perceive correctly nor act justly. Thus, however much the desire-led self may feel secure and comfortable in its world (9:38), its world is as weak as the house of the spider. The strength of its building material — the selfish thoughts and actions with which the self builds its world — is as flimsy and as destructible as the threads with which the spider's web is woven. To perceive the world through the spectacles of one's own desires is to perceive falsely and, consequently, to act unjustly. "And who goes farther astray," the Qur'an asks, "than he who follows his own desire without guidance from God?" (28:50).

8. *Ingratitude*. The believers turn from the "Way" of goodness and compassion because they forget God's mercies to them. The Qur'an calls such an act *kufr*, ingratitude, from the root *K F R*, meaning "to cover something."[18] The verb *kafara*, from the same root, is employed in the context of receiving favors and benefits to indicate covering up the fact of having received benefits. One becomes a *kafir*, that is, an ingrate, when one tries, in various ways, to cover up the fact of having received help from others. Such a person reserves for himself all the credit for his successes and shows no gratitude to others.

The Qur'an cites the example of one who was guilty (28:71) of ingratitude (28:82). Korah, the Qur'an says,

> was of Moses' folk, but he oppressed them; and We gave him treasures the keys of which weighed down a band of mighty men; his people said to him: 'Exult not, verily God loves not those who exult. And seek the abode of the hereafter with what God has given you, not forgetting your portion of this world; do good as God has done good to you, and seek not to cause corruption in the land; lo! God loves not those who cause corruption; he said: 'It has been given to me because of knowledge which I possess (28:78).

Korah's people saw that his forgetfulness of the good God had done from him led to both his pride in his own power and his oppressive behavior toward his fellow human beings; for in forgetting God's goodness to him, he forgot not only what true goodness is but also failed to do good for his fellow beings.

9. *Falsehood.* "Those who are ungrateful follow falsehood (*albatil*)" (47:3), the Qur'an says. To be ungrateful to God, in other words, is to engage in the act of lying; for when the believers fail to remember God's mercies to them, they begin to operate from a standpoint of denial of both God's and their fellow beings' goodness and compassion to themselves. Insofar as their thoughts and actions belie the fact of having received help from others, they are lies; and insofar as their world is created by such lies, it is constructed of falsehood.

Further, because the believers' forgetfulness of God's goodness makes the knowledge of "right conduct" (7:146) inaccessible to them, they are forced to depend on the knowledge provided by their senses and desires. They go "groping" on their faces (67:22) and "cling to the earth" (7:176) because they are uncertain of anything but that which can be grasped, touched, and ascertained by the five senses. However, because the knowledge acquired through the senses is distorted by desire, it is founded on "ignorance" (6:111) and "lack of (true) knowledge" (2:113). And judgments (45:21) based on such knowldege are, accordingly, mere "forgeries" (3:24), "inventions" (57:27), "creations" (7:191), "suppositions" (2:214), "surmises" (10:24; 41:22), outright "lies" (3:75), "conjectures" (51:10), and "guesses" (53:23).

10. *Fear and Sorrow.* Since "a guess can never take the place of the truth" (53:28), the misguided believers are enmeshed in "uncertainty" (45:32), "confusion" (2:42), "perplexity" (23:54), and "doubt" (22:5). The psychological effect of living in uncertainty and doubt is being harrowed by "fear" and "sorrow" (2:62). The practical effect of being lost in the darkness of uncertainty (45:32) is that the safety and well-being of their own physical beings become their foremost concern. They live their lives, the Qur'an says, as if they are caught in a

> rainstorm from the sky, wherein is darkness, thunder, and flash of lightning. They thrust their fingers in their ears by reason of the thunder-claps, for fear of death. . . .The lightning almost snatches away their sight from them. As often as it flashes forth for them they walk therein, and when it darkens against them they stand still. (2:19-20).

Therefore, God warns the believers, those who expend their resources and strive to build their world to fulfill their desires through falsehood, are like the person

> who founded his building on the brink of a crumbling, overhanging precipice so that it toppled with him into the fire of hell. The building which they built will never cease to be a misgiving in their hearts unless their hearts be torn to pieces" (9:109-110).

11. *Futility*. "Assuredly, if you ascribe partners (to God) your work will fail, and you will certainly be one of the losers" (39:65), the Qur'an says. In other words, the works of those who profess to believe in God but are really guided by their own desires "bear no fruit" (7:147). Even their "almsgiving," their spending of wealth in good causes (2:264), and their prayers, "go astray" (13:14); for whatever benefit they hope to attain through unjust means (or seemingly "good" acts) will turn out to be nothing but a "mirage" (24:39). Their works "are as ashes which the wind blows hard upon a stormy day" (14:18), or as "dust" upon a rock — "A rainstorm smites it, leaving it smooth and bare. They have no power over anything that they may have amassed" (2:264). And "that," the Qur'an says, "is the extreme failure" (14:18). Indeed.

> The likeness of that which they spend in this life of the world is as the likeness of a biting, icy wind which smites the harvest of a people who have been unjust to themselves, and devastates it. God was not unjust to them, but they were unjust to their own selves (3:117).

To remember God's mercies, then, is to believe in true "goodness" (92:6); to forget God's mercies is to "disbelieve in goodness" (92:9). Consequently, when the believers forget God's goodness and therefore lose sight of true goodness, they strive to possess the ornaments of this world — all the power, propserity, and enjoyment — in ways that only appear to be "good," but are, in fact, "unjust." Suffering from the illusion that they are autonomous beings, neither in need of anyone's guidance, nor accountable to anyone for their actions, the deluded believers are filled with insolence. And, goaded by their desires to find instant satisfaction, they, like a river out of control, swell and flow over their rightful boundaries. Thus, they refuse to acknowledge God's mercies to them and, like Korah, become followers of falsehood (40:78). Believers who follow in the footsteps of Korah, may, indeed, be called the true descendants of Korah. Such, the Qur'an points out, "do but plot against themselves though they perceive not" (6:123); for "God is not unjust to the people in anything; but the people do injustice to themselves" (10:44).

Conclusion. "Most of the people," the Qur'an says, "know only some appearance of the life of the world" (30:7). That is, their subjective desires show them only the outer world of existence — the world of delusions; remembrance of God's mercies, on the other hand, reveals to the believers the inner world of existence. It is as if those who remember God constantly and those who are oblivious of Him live and operate in two separate worlds — as, they will on the Judgment Day; "there will separate them a wall wherein is a gate, the inner side whereof contains compassion, while the outer side thereof is toward torment" (57:13). Those on the outer side will cry out to those who are on the inner side, "Were we not with you?" and they will be answered by those on the inner side, "Yes, verily, but you tempted one another, and hesitated, and doubted, and vain desires beguiled you" (57:14). To forget God's goodness is to live in the world of torment.

One cannot live in the world of desire and in the world of goodness at the same time, the Qur'an says, for God has not created two hearts in any human being (33:4). It cannot be that a human being can serve goodness with one heart and serve desire with another heart. Since a human being has only one heart, he or she cannot be preoccupied with, wholly committed to, two things (22:31). Whoever attempts to commit one's self equally to two things, "it is as if he had fallen from the sky and the birds had snatched him or the wind had blown him to a far off place" (22:31). That is, one will either be torn apart by conflicting loyalties, or one will lose control over one's life and not know who or where one is. Goodness and desire, love of the Hereafter and love of this world, selfgiving and greed, compassion and injustice cannot live together in the same heart. Human beings cannot serve both goodness and desire wholeheartedly.

The world of God and goodness and the world of desire and injustice are the inner and the outer worlds of existence. One cannot live at the same time in the world of light and in the world of darkness, in the world of knowledge and in the world of ignorance, in the world of certainty and in the world of uncertainty, in the world of reality and in the world of delusion. One must choose between the two. For those believers who, like Lot, choose to "migrate" (29:26) from the world in which God is forgotten to the world in which God is remembered constantly, and do "good deeds," the Qur'an says, "fear rests not upon them nor do they sorrow" (2:62).

Notes

I would like to express my gratitude to Dr. Waddi Haddad, Dr. R. Marston Speight, Dr. David Commins, Dr. Nan Hu, Mr. George H. Morrison, Mr. Timothy Adamson, and the Reverend Evelyn M. Weaver for making many insightful suggestions with regard to this article and for their constant support. Last, but not least, I am grateful to Dr. Andre´LaCocque, Director of the Center for Jewish-Christian Studies, without whose generous assistance and constant encouragement the conferences on the Middle Eastern religions at the Chicago Theological Seminary would not have been possible.

1. The English translation of the Qur'an used is *The Qur'an. Translated, with a critical re-arrangement of the Surahs*, by Richard Bell. Endinburgh: T & T Clark, 1960. I, II; reference to Qur'anic verses, however, are from *The Meaning of the Glorious Qur'an.* Translated by Muhammad M. Pickthall, Mecca: Muslim World League — Rabita, 1977.

2. Although the Qur'an uses the term "believers" most often to refer to Muslims — those who accepted Muhammad as their Prophet and the Qur'an as their revealed scripture — it often uses the same term to refer to all theists (2:177) of its times such as Zoroastrians, Jews, Christians, Sabaeans, Hanifs, and henotheists. The Qur'an defines a believer or a theist as one who "believes in God and the Last Day and sets things right" (2:62). On the other hand, the Qur'an calls many believers, or theists, "disbelievers" (la yu'minun, 10:101), "ingrates" (al-kafirun, 5:67), or "idolaters" (al-mushrikun, 4:51), not because they have renounced their belief in God but because, deep in their hearts, they love another being or thing more than God, or they deny accountability for their mode of existence (the Last Day), and, consequently, engage in acts of injustice towards their fellow beings. It is important to remember, then, that the Qur'anic charges of disbelief, idolatry (shirk), going astray (dalal), and ingratitude (kufr) are not leveled at non-Muslims and non-theists, but of those who are theists — Muslim and non-Muslim. It is these that the Qur'an constantly exhorts to "make religion pure" (4:146), that is, to actually practice what they profess to believe in.
3. The title of vicegerency implies a particular identity and function. A vicegerent is not an autonomous authority, but a representative of the authority from whom such title and power are derived. Consequently, a vicegerent acts, not on his own behalf, but on behalf of the authority he represents. In order to be a true vicegerent, he must faithfully carry out the objectives of the one who appointed him the vicegerent, not merely follow his own wishes. Similarly, a vicegerent of God subordinates himself to God and acts on behalf of God. He must transcend his own desires in order to fulfill God's wishes. And, as God is the symbol of all goodness, subordination to God is in effect commitment to goodness. To transcend the self, therefore, is to be in the state of goodness; to be possessed by the self is to be in the state of injustice.
4. "Mainly" because when it is not humanly possible to be compassionate and forgiving, seeking justice is "prescribed" (2:178; 5:,8, 45); "but," the Qur'an adds, "whosoever forgets (forgives), it shall be expiation for him" (5:45).
5. God, in the Qur'an, is presented primarily as the God of compassion and mercy, not of justice. His justice issues from His compassion. "If God were to take the people to task for their injustice," the Qur'an says, "He would not leave hereon a single living creature" (16:61), but "He has prescribed mercy as (incumbent) upon Himself" (6:12, 54). Therefore, "He reprieves them unto an appointed term" (35:45), so that "whoso does evil or wrongs himself, then seeks pardon of God, will find God forgiving, merciful" (4:110).
6. It also signifies the Qur'anic effort to keep the notions of compassion and mercy uppermost in the consciousness of the believers by reminding them, at the beginning of each Surah, that God's guidance for His creatures is conceived in the spirit of mercy and compassion. The believers should, accordingly, be guided by mercy and compassion in their dealings with each other.
7. The Qur'an insists, in other words, that one's relationship with one's fellow creatures is the *only* true expression of one's relationship with God; for, from the Qur'anic perspective, to do good for one's fellow human beings is to serve and worship God. It is true that there are many people who believe and act in goodness simply as a matter of principle, as a matter of self-integrity, and without any regard to personal gain and loss. They do not feel the need for the psychological and moral support that the notion of a deity gives others to prompt them to believe and act in goodness in a world where goodness more often than not fails and injustice almost always triumphs. However, for those who find themselves unable to believe and act in goodness without a belief in some deity, the Qur'anic insistence on the inseparability of belief and behavior is indeed of crucial importance. For this rea-

son, the Qur'an views the "believer" as one "who gives his wealth that he may purify himself; though to no one is he indebted. But (he gives) only out of desire for seeking the Face of his Lord Most High. He will be content" (92:18-21). It is no accident that the word for "almsgiving" (zaka, one of the Five Pillars of Islam) and the word for "purifying" oneself (tazakka) are derived from the same root, Z K W, which carries the basic meaning of growth or state of increase, augmentation (as a seed growing into fruition). The implication here is that self-growth is self-purification, and that self growth is possible only through self-giving, that is, through giving of one's energies, talents, resources — whatever God has given to one (5:48) — in doing good for others. It is "hastening" (sabaqa, 23:61) or "racing," as one does in a competitive race (istabaqa, 2:148; 5:48), to give when and where one sees the need (23:4), racing to protect oneself and others from harm (taqwa, 5:2), racing to set things right (islah, 20:75) — thus serving God through doing good for one's fellow human beings.

8. It is characteristic of the Qur'an to express any harm or good done to another as harm or good done to one's own self; and, therefore, whenever this notion is not explicitly stated, it is implied in all the admonitions to the believers throughout the Qur'an. See 2:272; 4:110; 6:104; 10:23, 44, 108; 17:7, 15; 27:40, 92; 29:6; 31:12; 35:18; 39:41; 41:46; 45:15; 47:38; 65:1.
9. The likeness of those believers who remain unaffected by their knowledge of true goodness, the Qur'an says, is "as the likeness of an ass carrying books" (62:5).
10. See Suras 12:42; 18:63: 20:94; 38:32; 87:6.
11. The Qur'an repeatedly warns the believers to guard against evil. Because evil is constantly on the offensive, visibly or invisibly, the believers must constantly strive to ward off its attacks. The Qur'an uses the word taqwa, which means putting something between oneself and the thing that is attacking in order to protect, preserve, and defend oneself against its harm. Izutsu says, "Ittaqa means that you place between yourself (A) and something you are afraid of (B), something (C) which might protect you by preventing it (B) from reaching you. In short, it means self-defence by means of something. The general situation is this: A man (A) perceives something (B) coming towards him, which looks dangerous, destructive, or at least harmful. He does not like it to reach him; he must stop it before it reaches him and does harm to him, so he puts between himself and the thing (B) something (C) which is enough to stop its oncoming." Toshihiko Izutsu, *God and Man in the Qur'an. Semantics of the Qur'anic Weltanschauung* (Tokyo, Japan: Keio University, 1964), p. 235.
12. Toshihiko Izutsu, *Ethico-Religious Concepts in the Qur'an* (Montreal, Canada: McGill University Press, 1966), pp. 133-134. See also E. W. Lane, *Arabic-English Lexicon* (Cambridge, England: The Islamic Texts Society, 1984), Originally published in 1877. II, p. 1798.
13. In distinguishing between the "losers" and the "prosperers" among the theists, the Qur'an says: "Some are unjust to themselves, some moderate, some outstrip others through good deeds" (35:32). The losers are those who are "unjust to themselves"; in the Heareafter they will be "on the left hand" (56:9). The prosperers consist of two kinds: 1) those who are moderate, that is, those who sincerely strive to do good works; they will be "on the right hand" of God, and 2) those who "outstrip others through good deeds" and are "foremost in the race" (56:10); they will be brought near (unto God)" (56:11).
14. Toshihiko Izutsu, *Ethico-Religious Concepts in the Qur'an*, p. 165. See also E. W. Lane, *Arabic-English Lexicon* II, p. 1920.
15. Izutsu says that tagha refers to the phenomenon of "water rising so high as to exceed the bounds and overflow the banks." T. Izutusu, *Ethico-Religous Concepts in the Qur'an* , p. 149. See also E. W. Lane, *Arabic-English Lexicon*, p. 1856.

16. The Qur'an, unlike traditional Islam, does *not* dwell on the oneness of God or tawhid, but on the believer's love of and total commitment to God. "Of the people are some, " the Qur'an says, "who take into themselves rivals to God, loving (hubb) them with a love like that given to God; only those who believe love God with a stronger love" (2:165). The Qur'anic criterion for distinguishing between the believer and the unbeliever is thus not based on such a simple formula as belief in the oneness of God (tawhid), but on loving or not loving God more than any other being or thing. For the Qur'an it is not the kind of belief one has about God but the kind of relationship one has with God that is ultimately important. That is the crucial test of a believer or non-believer. As the Qur'an clearly says: "only those who believe love God with a stronger love" than they love other beings or things. The Qur'an does not say that human beings should not love any being or thing except God; it only says that they should not love any being or thing more than God. Those who do not love God with a love stronger than their love for other beings or things are, therefore, not believers. Those whose love for the "ornaments of this world," for power, prosperity, and material enjoyment, for uniqueness, for Zoroaster, Abraham, Jesus, and Muhammad, for rabbis, priests, and Saints, for Lat, Manat, and Uzza and other gods of their fancies exceeds their love for God, such, the Qur'an says, are those who are guilty of ascribing partners to God (al-mushrikun) regardless of what they call themselves— Zoroastrians, or Jews, or Christians, or Sabaeans, or Muslims, or henotheists. To love any being or thing more than God is to take another patron (59:63), helper (30:39), advisor (7:21), protector (10:27), or guardian (17:2) in addition to God. Thus those theists who profess to believe in God but in actuality serve their own materialistic desires are the real idolaters (al-mushrikun) and ingrates (al-kafirun). To love some thing or being more than God, then, from the Qur'anic point of view, is to be a disbeliever. Most theists (believers in God) are thus seen as disbelievers (2:100; 3:110; 5:49; 6:116; 26:118, 121, 139). Consequently, the most fundamental distinction between the believer and the disbeliever to be found in the Qur'an is between those who remember God constantly and those who are forgetful of Him, between those who desire God and those whose god is desire. The Qur'anic contention is that a theist cannot be a true believer without the constant remembrance of God, for to remember God constantly is to remember his goodness, and to remember His goodness is to do good to one's fellow human beings. The ideal believer, thus, is one who wholly commits (aslama) his or her self to the service of God; and, isasmuch as God stands for goodness, the ideal believer is one who believes in the ways of goodness and wholly commits his or her self to the service of goodness. That is true commitment (islam) and the true way of being (din al-qayyimati, 98:5). Obviously, not all believers, that is, those who sincerely love God more than any other thing or being, are able to remember God and His goodness at all times. From time to time, the believers, even those who are prophets, are distracted from the remembrance of God and His goodness for various reasons. Consequently, the Qur'an assures all believers by saying that God does not "tax any self beyond its scope" (2:233), for "He is best aware of you (from the time) when He created you from the earth, and when you were hidden in the bellies of your mothers" (53:32). Therefore, the Qur'an says, "there is no fault in you if you make mistakes, but only in what your hearts premeditate" (33:5), and "those who avoid enormities of sin and indecencies, save the unwilled offenses (for them) lo! your Lord is of vast mercy" (53:32).
17. "Good deeds refer to those unselfish, responsible, and charitable acts which, while upholding the right of all concerned, contribute to the "improvement" (islah) and "protection" (taqwa) (see 5:93) of one's fellow human beings and the environment in which one lives.

18. T. Izutsu, *Ethico-Religious Concepts in the Qur'an*, pp. 119-120. See also E. W. Lane, *Arabic-English Lexicon* . II, p. 2620.

IV

Approaches to Islam

BY WILLEM A. BIJLEFELD

While honestly and deeply grateful for the opportunity to share today's events with you, I must also confess that the topic graciously assigned to me fills me with fear and trembling — mainly because I am not sure what I am supposed to speak about. That ambiguity was perhaps intentional. During my stay in Egypt for the past several weeks, the organizers may have decided that this was a good title exactly because it would give me the freedom to talk about anything I wanted. I greatly appreciate that kindness, but one of my weaknesses is that as soon as a title is formulated, it begins in some way or another to mesmerize me, and the greater the unclarity, the harder I try to guess what those who formulated it meant with it and what those who saw it announced expect from it.

"Approaches to Islam" is bound to mean very different things to different people. Most of you no doubt have read it as: approaches to the study of Islam. Two titles are sufficient to illustrate the wide spectrum of topics and issues that fall under this category: von Grunebaum's 1970 article, "Approaching Islam — A Digression," an early and rather extensive critique of the approach of Kenneth Cragg,[1] and the collection of essays, *Approaches to Islam in Religious Studies*, edited by Richard Martin,[2] a volume that contains several important contributions and that reaches, in my opinion, its climax in the concluding chapter by Professor Fazlur Rahman.[3]

But there are, no doubt, also some who anticipate a discussion of various, mainly Christian, "approaches to Islam," a survey of the long and complex history of Western attitudes towards Islam. A few may even have realized that the "approach" terminology seems to mark a not unimportant shift in Christian missionary thinking in this century in which we moved in the forties from mission to (among, on behalf of) the Muslim world to the language of a "Christian Approach to Islam (or to Muslims)," a terminology that, in the fifties and sixties, was replaced in many circles by the word "encounter with," and from the early seventies onward by "dialogue with" Muslims.[4] Did these changes reflect an ever growing awareness of Muslims as "partners," a steadily growing sense of mutuality, or were they changes in wording only? Kurshid Ahmad no doubt voiced the opinion of many Muslims when he remarked in 1976, "the Muslims feel that the names have changed but that the substance has not."[5] Christian perspectives on Islam and Christian-Muslim relations are so diverse, also at the moment, that Ahmad's remarks cannot simply be either affirmed or denied.

With due respect for what some may have anticipated, a half hour survey of old and new, changing and stubbornly surviving "Christian" perspectives on Islam in the past four centuries or from the very beginning of our co-existence onward, seems dreadfully unattractive and totally superfluous. Excellent material is available: Norman Daniel's by now "classic" study, *Islam and the West*,[6] and many of his later works, especially, *Islam, Europe and Empire*[7]; the extensive documentation of Muslim and Christian polemical writings, reflecting a great diversity of attitudes and evaluations, made available by Gaudeul;[8] and — just one more title out of the many available — Maxime Rodinson's *Europe and the Mystique of Islam*,[9] an eighty page survey of Western views of the Muslim world (ending with a section on the birth of Orientalism in the Enlightenment), followed by a fifty pages long discussion of the beginning of a new approach to Arab and Islamic Studies (concluding with proposals for future study.)[10]

Because we are here today at the gracious invitation of Chicago Theological Seminary and honored by the presence of visitors from some other seminaries in this city, it seems appropriate to focus our attention as far as the study of Islam is concerned on the place of this field of academic inquiry at a theological seminary and/or within the contest of a broadly conceived religious studies program. One of the first and most crucial questions we need to face is the one repeatedly and sometimes passionately raised especially, but not only, by Muslims: can Islam be taught appropriately by anyone who is not a Muslim? The insiders vs. outsiders issue seems particularly urgent in this specific field, but it is obviously one of much wider scope. Although many in our society may be inclined to dismiss offhand any suggestion of faculty appointments (and student admissions?) in which religious affiliations would play a decisive role, we need to take the question seriously. Centuries of painfully distorted images of Islam in the West have led to a widespread distrust in what "Westerners" (Christians and secularists, missionaries and communists) can accomplish in this area. But beyond these specifics, is it not true that an understanding from within always has priority over an understanding from outside that particular religious tradition and community? The answer to this last question is not unanimous, and while those who reserve ultimate validity only for insiders' perspectives and interpretations still seem to dominate much of the discussion, the number of those who challenge this assumption is definitely growing. Most of the answers given are ultimately determined by a person's understanding of "the study of religion" as an academic field. In the early seventies, Michael Novak's *Ascent of the Mountain, Flight of the Dove: An Invitation to Religious Studies* sparked a lively discussion. Novak declared:

> Religious studies are to a dangerous degree personal. They call for an attitude of a fresh awareness and a new sensitivity to others, to nature and to oneself, a series of conversations in one's way of life. For what is the point of merely studying *about* religion without also changing one's life.?[12]

"Religious Studies" seems for him to come close to a kind of religious exercise, and "being religious" could be understood to be a condition for fruitful involvement in teaching (and studying) in this area. As far as the inner-outsider question is concerned, the author is very cautious but ultimately maintains the priority of the insiders-perspective while making a crucial distinction between an "insider" and a "communicant:"

> It can happen that a person's specialized knowing has little to do with his actual living. An atheist may be the world's greatest expert in the history of Buddhism or Christianity. Yet perhaps nowhere more than in the field of religious studies does disharmony between a person's knowledge and his personal living invite students to be sad.[13]
>
> Granted, it is not true that only a Buddhist can teach Buddhist studies. Granted, it is not true that a man teaching Roman Catholic studies should be "a spokesman for Catholicism ..." Yet it *is* true that a religion is a way of life, rather than a set of rituals, a creed, a set of truth claims.
>
> The sole road to understanding a religion is not external, objective, academic. On the contrary, professionals need to know the limits of their own personal voyage, the distorting effects of these limits — and how to enter vicariously (both critically and sympathetically) into the voyages of others who differ from them in person and in culture. There is a way of becoming an "insider" without being a "communicant." If it is not a complete or total way, it is fruitful and enlarging for the one who stubbornly attempts its ascents or is borne up by serendipity. And it makes claims to "academic detachment" suspect: What *sort* of detachment? And, *Why?*[14]

Whatever our disagreements with Novak may be, it seems important to hear his warnings against a solely "external, objective, academic" approach to the study of any religion and his questioning of the notion of "academic detachment" in this field — important not the least because it may help some of us to understand more fully the Muslim reactions I referred to earlier. That certain aspects of the study of a religion (its history, e.g.) may be open to outsiders, while other dimensions can only be placed safely in the hands of insiders, is an oft-repeated suggestion. Although not explicitly stated this way, one senses it present in, e.g., Muhammad Abdul Rauf's chapter "Outsiders' Interpretations of

Islam: A Muslim's Point of View.[15] Whereas the social and historical dates of any religion can be studied alike by anyone, atheist or theist, believer or unbeliever, there are, in Evans-Pritchard's words, other dimensions in which the approach of the believers and unbelievers go in different directions: "For both, religion is part of social life, but for the believer it has also another dimension."[16] Can a person who does not belong to a particular religious community fully understand and faithfully interpret that other dimension? Can she or he become, at least to a high degree, an "insider" without being a "communicant?" Is it possible to suspend, to "bracket" one's own perspectives and judgements and to live oneself into those of people living in another religious tradition and community? This is not the place and time to enter into the still ongoing discussion on *epoche*, and it must suffice simply to state that many of those who fully acknowledge the merits of this call to a bracketing of one's own views and convictions are also aware of the serious questions that surround it. Is *epoche* not too frequently presented as a kind of spiritual exercise rather than as a sober hermeneutic device? Is there not the proven danger that it is exactly this suspension of judgment that allows many people to persevere in their very negative assessment of other religious traditions they are studying? Rather than allowing their growing acquaintance with other people of faith to have an impact on their own understanding of God and history, of the world and of the meaning of (religious) pluralism, they emerge unchanged from their temporary abandonment of judgment. As a warning against an insensitive and prejudiced approach to the study of Islam and as a reminder of the need to move beyond an "objective" study of the externals of that tradition, the provocative appeal an outstanding German missiologist of the middle of this century, Walter Freytag, made to a group of Christian missionaries, was and remains extremely important:

> You have not really understood another religious tradition than your own unless you have been tempted by the insights of that religion.

But would it be possible for a Christian momentarily to respond, in obedience and with gratitude, to the call of the mu'ezzin and then to stand up and approach Islam (the Muslims) in an even more "hardened" way than ever before? At any rate, Freytag's words were intended as a very personal appeal and, obviously, not as the formation of a criterion to be applied in judging the academic adequacy of anyone's performance in Islamic (Hindu, Buddhist), Studies. More or less as a conclusion to his discussion of the insider-outsider issue — in the context of which he cautioned against any illusions about the possibility really to feel and live oneself into another religious tradition — Frazlur Rahman offered the following concise delineation of the conditions for and the character of a meaningful academic study of a religion:

> Let us emphasize that the kind of intellectual understanding being considered — given concern, sympathy, and lack of prejudice — is a sort of scientific knowledge. *It is not a religious exercise but a quasi-scientific (intellectual) knowledge of religious experience, where the normativeness or authority of the experience vanishes, but*

> *something of its direct effect upon the experiencing subject (including the latter's report of it) can be preserved and made accessible to others.* The experience as a living and integral whole, therefore, cannot be conveyed by an historian or social scientist; such scholars nonetheless can appreciate it intellectually and convey it so that it becomes a part of "scientific knowledge." (italics mine)[17]

Here the insider-outsider distinction remains valid, and the limits of any outsider's "understanding" are acknowledged; but as far as academic intellectual understanding is concerned, outsiders are seen as potentially full participants in the study and interpretation of a religious tradition.

A final question that arises in this connection is whether also with regard to the insider-outsider issue a distinction needs to be made between religious studies departments and theological schools. On this continent, some of the latter function in very much the same way as the former do, but in many other parts of the world the difference in function and objectives is far more pronounced. There the seminaries seem to assume a certain degree of commonality (especially as far as the faculty is concerned) in response to what a specific religious community holds to be the ultimate truth, whereas university programs in religious studies are in principle open to faculty (and students) of any or without any particular religious commitment. In the mid seventies, in a conversation I had with a few administrators and faculty members at Aligarh Muslim University, there seemed to be agreement that while the faculty of theology (obviously: "Islamic theology") was open to Muslims only, they welcomed others, especially Christians, to enroll in the program in Islamic Studies. Since there is often particularly with regard to Qur'anic Studies an overt hesitation to entrust this field to anyone but a Muslim, this may be a good instance to raise the question whether the same guidelines should apply at a (Muslim) theological institution and a religious studies department. In his earlier mentioned article dealing with outsiders' interpretations of Islam, Muhammad Abdul-Rauf wrote:

> Being the Word of God to man recited in prescribed diction and sounds, the Holy Qur'an is inimitable and not subject to the limiting dimensions of space and time. The order of its verses in each of its 114 chapters, which are mutually and closely related, cannot be subjected to limits imposed by conceptions of finitude.[18]

While this kind of statement might well serve as a shared conviction at a particular theological institution, it is difficult to see how its affirmation could be made into a condition and prerequisite for a meaningful participation in Qur'anic Studies within the context of a religious studies program.

Inadequate and unfinished as these marginal notes on the insider-outsider issue are, we need to move to three other issues on which we want to touch.

Following upon remarks made by Professor Fazlur Rahman this morning, I would like to suggest that at many of our Western (especially our Christian) institutions, one of the most serious weaknesses in our offerings in Islamic Studies has been and is the tendency to separate the study of the message of the

Qur'an from the study of the life and work of the Prophet Muhammad. To offer a "Life of Muhammad" without constant references to the Message that determined his Prophethood seems totally unsatisfactory, if not seriously misleading. Interrelating the two subjects should not mean, on the other hand, reducing the Qur'an to being the product of the Prophet's mind. The Qur'an is a "given," and no matter how different the interpretations of that notion may be, it is among us as a treasure "received," for anyone of us, whatever our religious commitments are — *at least* in the sense of being "received" from the community of faith that has appropriated this sacred text,in a variety of ways, from one generation to another.

The second issue on which I want to touch is that in many at first sight very "positive" observations about Islam — statements that, indeed, contrast sharply with the bitterly hostile remarks of the past — many Christians are answering their own theological questions and are not only in *that* sense "responding" to Islam. For example, a number of Christians nowadays wholeheartedly acknowledge the prophethood of Muhammad in as far as they assign him a "pre-Christian" prophetic role, parallel to that of the Old Testament prophets. Whatever one may think about the validity of this statement as an answer to the *Christian* question where to place Muhammad in God's history of salvation, it confuses the Muslim-Christian dialogue if this answer is offered as an at least partial recognition of the Islamic affirmation of Muhammad's prophetic role. No matter how many Christians have suggested this for at least the past eight centuries,[19] the Qur'an does not present Muhammad as a messenger only to the Arabs who up to that time had been deprived of access to the prophetic revelation, and "dating" him (as some Christians have done) as belonging to the pre-Mosaic stage of God's history of revelation is not an halfway affirmation of the Qur'anic proclamation but a rejection of it. My point here is *not* the validity or the fallacy of this thesis from a Christian point of view — the point I am making is, simply, that Christians should not be surprised and disappointed if these and similar well-intended "positive" statements about Islam are sharply resented by many Muslims and seldom, if ever, serve as bridge builders.

Of an entirely different nature is the third and last issue I want to mention. While it is a welcome development if one or more courses on Islam are added to a theological or religious studies program that is primarily concerned with the Jewish or Christian religious tradition, the full potential for significant enrichment is not realized until and unless Islamic data are (also) adequately introduced and seriously considered within the framework of several other courses in various fields, especially — at a Christian seminary — Biblical Studies, Historical and Systematic Theology, and Ethics. Today I can only hint at what I have in mind by making a few brief and somewhat disconnected suggestions. What better starting point — *in this context* — to raise the highly significant issue of "history and revelation" than a close and careful study of the role and function of the historical narratives in the Hebrew Scriptures, the New Testament and the Qur'an? Abdoldjavad Falaturi's remark: "there is no reason to conceive of revelation as something temporal or historical,"[20] could well serve as the basis for a very valuable discussion of diverse views on the revelation and history issue. "To the claim of Küng that both Christians and Muslims believe in God as the historical God, I would respond in the negative,"[21] Seyyed Hossein Nasr wrote in his important comments on Hans Küng's Harvard Divinity School lecture in 1984.[22] Placing this observation alongside Ulrich Mann's statement *"der Gott der Christenheit ist ganz und gar geschichtlich"*[23] ("The God of Christianity is totally historical") would add interesting material for a significant discussion. Within the realm of Biblical and Qur'anic Studies, Fazlur Rahman's statement about "election" made this morning[24] could lead to an in depth exploration of what the wider implications are of these differences and to a discussion of the issue of "particularism and universalism" in our three sacred scriptures. Moving to some also arbitrarily chosen illustrations from the New Testament field, Christological statements such as the two that follow would give ample opportunity for a meaningful discussion of this dimension of Christian-Muslim relationships. Pointing to an important point of contact with Qur'anic Christology (clearly without claiming that Qur'anic Christology is somehow identical with that of Luke), Räisänen stressed "the emphatic subordination of Jesus to God" in St. Luke's Gospel.[25] And in a discussion of Biblical perspectives on the meaning of Christ's death and the notion of reconciliation, Berkhof suggested — a remark made without any reference to Muslim points of view — that it seems "preferable in our time not to interpret Jesus' death primarily and exclusively with the, to us, rather foreign Pauline, juridical and cultic concepts ... but rather with the Johannine concepts of love, obedience and glorification."[26] In the area of Historical Theology, it would not be without interest — particularly in largely Muslim environments in Africa and Asia — to include data from Muslim apologetics in a discussion of partripassianism and theopaschitism. And what do Muslims hear us say when those of us who are Christians speak about the "suffering" of God and God's "vulnerability"?

As far as the field of Ethics is concerned, the growing concern with social ethics and public policy issues is of the greatest importance and may help many "outsiders" to begin to grasp the reasons for Muslims' insistence of the crucial significance of the shari'a as an integral dimension of Islam.

In all of this, uncritical "discoveries" of parallels are as counterproductive as premature conclusions about mutually exclusive positions. Similarities, analogies, and contrasts will need to be identified in a series of patient and careful comparative studies. To remain, in this process, open to the joy of recognition of what unites us is as vitally important as to resist the temptation of sacrificing what is distinctive in our traditions in order to enlarge the "common ground" on which we are supposed to stand.

At the beginning we talked about different meanings of the term "approaches to Islam." In a postscript even more unscientific than all that preceded it, I want to return to the word "approach" once more, in a very personal way, at a different level than that of probing some questions related to the academic study of Islam. At one point in this presentation we touched upon possible differences between religious studies programs and theological seminaries as far as the outsider-insider issue is concerned. Whatever may be true for our theological *institutions*, is it not time that we begin to take seriously the truth that "as far as *theology* is the concern, there are no outsiders" (Kenneth Cragg). The devotional depth of the words "our God" is as undeniable as the danger of the use of this pronoun with a "possessive" connotation that seems to exclude others from the circle of God's children. And "approach" so easily carries with it the connotation of a distance that must be bridged over, the notion of "we" vs. "you." Can we, as Muslims and Christians, begin to think in different terms than that of an approach to each other, and rather understand our relationship in terms of a common pilgrimage to God, a pilgrimage not *out* of this world, but, *for God's sake, into* this world. Sometimes we will recognize with immense gratitude how close to each other we walk on the same path. At other points our ways will divide, now and then painfully so. But even then we rest assured that we move in the same direction. For "to God is our return." And no matter how pressing many of our unanswered questions are, in the end God will judge between us regarding the matters in which we differ (cf. S. 3:55). "Now I know in part; then I shall understand fully, even as I have been fully understood" (1 Corinthians 13:12). In the light of this eschatological perspective we now turn back, with humility and inner reserve, to what faces us today and tomorrow, resolved anew really to "give" ourselves to be understood and to understand each other more fully.

Notes

1. G.E. von Grunebaum, "Approaching Islam: A Digression," *Middle Eastern Studies*, VI (1970), 127-49.
2. Richard C. Martin, ed., *Approaches to Islam in Religious Studies*. Tucson: The University of Arizona Press, 1985.
3. "Approaches to Islam in Religious Studies. Review Essay," Ibid., pp. 189-202, 233-34.
4. For a fuller discussion, see my forthcoming article "Rethinking Missions: The Church and the World of Islam in the Twentieth Century," to be published in *The Muslim World*, LXXXI (1991).
5. At the "Christian Mission and Islamic Da'wah" Conference of 1976; see *In. Rev. of Mission*, LXV, no. 260 (1976), 446.
6. Norman Daniel, *Islam and the West*. Edinburgh: The University Press, 1960.
7. Norman Daniel, *Islam, Europe and Empire*. Edinburgh: The University Press, 1966.
8. Jean-Marie Gaudeul, *Encounters and Clashes: Islam and Christianity in History*. Rome: Pontificio Istituto di Studi Arabi e Islamici, 1984, 2 volumes.
9. Maxime Rodinson, *Europe and the Mystique of Islam*. Trans. by Roger Veinus. Seattle: Distributed by The University of Washington Press, 1987.
10. Although some of his observations may be as controversial as those of his earlier publication *Mohammed* (first French edition 1961; translated by Anne Carter, first edition 1971; New York: Random House, Vintage Books, 1974), this survey concise and in many parts extremely insightful, deserves serious attention.
11. Michael Novak, *Ascent of the Mountain, Flight of the Dove: An Invitation to Religious Studies*. New York: Harper & Row, 1971.
12. Ibid., p. XI.

13. Ibid., pp. XII-XIII.
14. Michael Noval, "The Identity Crisis of Us All: Response to Professor Crouter," *J.A.A.R.*, XL (1972), 77. Richard E. Crouter's article, "Michael Novak and the Study of Religion," ibid., 55-64.
15. In *Approaches to Islam*, pp. 179-88.
16. E.E. Evans-Pritchard, *Theories of Primitive Religion* (Oxford: Clarendon Press, 1965), p. 121.
17. In *Approaches to Islam*, pp. 193-94.
18., Ibid., pp. 186-87.
19. A well-known twelfth century example is found in Paul of Antioch's "Letter to One of His Muslim Friends in Sidon," section 7. See Paul Khoury, *Paul d'Antioche. Évêque Melkite de Sidon* (XII e s.) (Beyrouth: Imprim. Catholique, n.d.), p. 170 (French translation), p. 61 (Arabic text).
20. Annemarie Schimmel and Abdoldjavad Falaturi, eds., *We Believe in One God: The Experience of God in Christianity and Islam* (New York: Seabury Press, 1979), p. 66 (in an article, "Experience of Time of History in Islam").
21. Seyyed Hossein Nasr, "Response to Hans Küng's Paper on Christian-Muslim Dialogue," *The Muslim World*, LXXVII (1987), 102.
22. Hans Küng, "Christianity and World Religions: The Dialogue With Islam as One Model," *The Muslim World*, LXXVII (1987), 80-95.
23. Ulrich Mann, *Das Christentum als absolute Religion* (Darmstadt: Wissenschaftliche Buchgesellschaft, 1971), pp. 44-45.
24. Cf. also his remarks in *Major Themes of the Qur'an* (Minneapolis-Chicago: Bibliotheca Islamica, 1980), pp. 165-55 ("the whole tenor of the Qur'anic argument is against election").
25. Heikki Räisänen, "The Portrait of Jesus in the Qur'an. Reflections of a Biblical Scholar," *The Muslim World*, LXX (1980), 127-29.
26. H. Berkhof, *Christian Faith*, translated by S. Woudstra (Grand Rapids: Eerdmans, 1979), p. 305.

V

The Universal Horizon of Biblical Particularism

BY JON D. LEVENSON

This article is reprinted here with the kind permission of the American Jewish Committee, and of the author. (First published in Jewish Perspective, April 1985).

I. The Ambiguities of "Universalism"

There is probably nothing in Judaism that has attracted as much attention and generated as much controversy as the biblical idea that Jews are the Chosen People. There were pagan authors in antiquity who resented what they saw as Jewish exclusiveness, and early Christianity claimed to universalize the Hebrew Bible's parochial view of the divine covenant, making it available to all the nations of the earth. Anti-Semitism has historically focused on alleged Jewish clannishness, and has charged that Jews' absorption with their own group leads to lack of concern for others. In response, many Jews have stressed the universalism inherent in prophetic ethics, downplaying evidence of Jewish particularism in the Bible. Other Jews, in the aftermath of the Holocaust, have reasserted and exaggerated the uniqueness of the Jewish people, even to the extent of denying the applicability to Jews of the outside world's moral standards.

Given this long history of polemics and apologetics, it is no easy task to sort out the biblical material on universalism and Jewish particularism in a scholarly way. But such an exercise is needed, not only to help non-Jews overcome confusion and bigotry about Judaism, but also to enable Jews to understand their own biblical heritage and its contemporary implications, for, as we shall see, the all-too-common contrast between "universal" and "particularistic" religion is simplistic, grossly misleading, and even dangerous.

Predicated of a religious tradition, the term "universalism" can carry a number of divergent meanings. It may simply refer to the universality of the deity: No other god exists, and the whole world, without exception, is his. Such universalism, however, still allows for pockets of particularism. Although God may be lord of the world, he need not care about the world in its entirety, or he may care about different classes of creatures in different measures. He may, for example, favor persons over animals, although he is the creator of both, and even permit persons to kill animals without incurring guilt, but not the reverse. Or, he may single out one set of persons rather than another — such as the people of Israel, the Christian Church, or the Islamic *ummah* — for special favors and special responsibilites.

When this is held to have happened, hard questions have to be faced. What is the relationship of those who have not been so singled out to the universal deity and to his special group? The outsider may be condemned as an offense to the universal lord whom he does not acknowledge, or he may be respected as a person of dignity who is not to blame for his status. Or, again, he may be regarded as a person of diminished dignity whose true worth can be realized only by his electing to join the favored sub-group. Religious traditions that affirm both a universal God and a particular group as his elect face an especially difficult challenge on the question of moral standards and accountability. Has the God of all imparted knowledge of his ethical norms to those who have not experienced his revelation? If so, how? And what is the relationship of the universal ethical norms, if they exist, to the norms that govern the favored sub-group? If these two sets of norms are identical, then one can speak of a *moral* universalism that has been disclosed only to a special group: everyone should observe one group's ethic. In this case, the particular religious tradition will tend to identify itself with humanness itself, and to imply either the subhumanity of outsiders or their unwitting practice of the insider's religion, or both. There is another alternative: some norms oblige all persons, and others oblige only the sub-group. Here, universalism is affirmed on one tier, and particularism on another.

Although some religious traditions may on occasion conceive of themselves as representing or answering to a universal human condition, as a matter of historical fact, all religious traditions are particular, since none includes everyone. There is no evidence that mankind has ever had only one religion. Religion is as much a creature of culture as it is of nature, and human culture is particular. To be sure, while no religion is universal, some aspire to be. In this sense, a "universal religion" may mean simply one that accepts proselytes, that is, one that is willing or eager to extend its particularity indefinitely. Or it may signify one that is found in a large number of different cultures. In this cse, the term "universal" is misleading, since the religion has not transformed a highly diverse humanity into one universal body. Instead, it has formed symbiotic relationships with various enduring particularisms. The variety of human cultures has been eroded but not overcome, and there is no reason to assume that the erosion is irreversible, since few things are more characteristic of human experience than the fragmentation and disintegration of overarching structures of beliefs.

Yet another understanding of "universalism" may teach that in some future consummation, human variety will disappear altogether or submit permanently to an all-inclusive structure. In this case, particularism may be predicated of the present aeon, and universalism of the next. There is no contradiction between *historical* particularism and *eschatological* universalism, limited or total.

II. The Universality of God and the Dignity of Man

Before we attempt to determine where the Hebrew Bible fits into this rude typology of universalisms and particularisms, we must first acknowledge frankly that there is no one "biblical" position on this or on most other great theological issues. The Bible is an anthology of writings composed over a period of about a thousand years, in several lands, and by authors of various sorts. It presents a spectrum of positions, and although the spectrum is not endless, neither is it so limited as to facilitate generalization. Intellectual honesty requires us to avoid the popular tactic of citing a passage that appeals to us as if it were the entirety of the tradition. Though the temptation to read our own values unto the text is nearly overpowering, it must be resisted; complete objectivity is not humanly possible, but it remains a necessary ideal.

In spite of its anthological character, in Judaism the Hebrew Bible (especially the Torah, its first five books) is considered a coherent entity, not merely a concatenation of incompatibles. This postulate of coherence enables us to regard the separate elements as parts of a total picture that may not in reality have been affirmed by their original authors. Thus, some systematic statement is possible, so long as it is loose enough to allow for exceptions and self-aware enough to acknowledge its dependence on a canon that did not exist in the biblical period itself.

Universalism in the sense of the universality of the deity is most striking in those biblical traditions that speak of God as the creator of the world. The placement of the story of comsic creation by God (*'elohim*) at the beginning of the entire Bible (Gen. 1:1-2:4a) establishes a universal horizon for the particular story of Israel, which occupies most of the rest of that sacred book. Especially noteworthy is the lack of all spatial locality in that account of creation. Unlike the following creation story, that of the creation of Adam and then Eve by the Lord God (*YHWH 'elohim*, Gen. 2:4b-24), this first account mentions no landmarks, no countries, no rivers, not even a Garden of Eden. Instead, men and women, created together, exist on undifferentiated dry land. No spot on earth can claim the prestigious status of primordiality: There is no "place" at which creation began and where its energies may yet be available. The familiar world is entirely and evenly the consequence of the creative act.

Here, it is instructive to contrast a Babylonian creation story, the *Enuma Elish*, in which Marduk's creation of the world culminates in the construction of Babylon, his city and therefore the capital of the cosmos, and of Esagila, its temple and his palace.[1] Like *'elohim*, Marduk is also a cosmic creator-god; his power is not limited to Babylon.[2] But, as is emphatically not the case in Gen. 1:1-2:4a, his special realtionsihip to a particular community is embedded in the very structure of cosmic order.

In the biblical story, the only *particular* vestige of the act of creation is a cultic rite, the Sabbath, through which man replicates the rhythm of the protological events (2:1-3).[3] In this sense, the Sabbath is as universal as the deity whom man imitates, despite the fact that it is disclosed to Israel alone, and not until the generation of Moses (Exod. 20:8-11). In short, the "prestige of origins"[4] applies not to something so particular as a place, but to a way of organizing something universal — time. Like Esagila, the Sabbath recollects the divine repose after the work of creation, but in a nonspatial and therefore universalizable way. Unlike the *Enuma Elish*, Gen. 1:1-2:4a does not serve to buttress any particular political or cultic order.

It is also highly significant that in both creation accounts at the beginning of Genesis (1:1-2:4a and 2:4b-24), it is humanity in general and not any people in particular that is created. Israel is not primordial. It emerges in history, twenty generations after the creation of the human species in the image of God (or the gods, 1:26-27). "Israel," in the words of a contemporary scholar, "has no particular supernatural status by birth and early history."[5] It is neither descended from the gods nor divine itself. All people are created equal, in the divine image. The creation stories in Genesis serve as a powerful warrant for a Jewish doctrine of human brotherhood and as a formidable obstacle to any attempt to mix Judaism and racism.

The relatedness of the members of the human family to each other and to God is underscored and formalized in the announcement of an eternal covenant with Noah in Gen. 9:1-17. Underlying this covenant is a theology that places all peoples in a relationship of grace and accountability with God. The subsequent estalishment of covenants with all Abrahamites (Genesis 17) and with all Israelites (Exodus 24) is to be read against the background of this universal covenant. Israel's relationship to God is thus both unique and universal: no other people has it, yet all humanity has something of the same order.

The Noahide Covenant, which is mentioned nowhere else in the Hebrew Bible, assumes greater importance in rabbinic Judaism, where it serves as the functional equivalent of natural law, specifying the seven commandments incumbent upon all humanity, Jew and gentile alike.[6] The greater role of the Noahide Covenant in rabbinic than in biblical Judaism calls into question the too common notion that the rabbis abandoned the universal dimension of biblical theology and retreated into a cocoon of ethnocentricity. Indeed, one of the reasons for the absence of a missionary thrust in rabbinic theology is the doctrine of the dignity of man in general, whether Israelite or not. Those who think outsiders can have a proper relationship with God as they are will feel less of an impulse to make them into insiders.

It is significant that the primeval history (Genesis 1-11) presents mankind as primordially monotheistic and, in fact, YHWHistic (4:26). Idolatry, which, according to the rabbis, violates a Noahide commandment, is not intrinsic to man, and a gentile is not assumed to be idolatrous. It is possible to be a faithful and responsible worshipper of YHWH (the proper name of the God of Israel) without being an Israelite. In this, the YHWHistic source in the primeval history goes beyond even the universalism of Gen. 9:1-17, derived from the priestly source (P), which maintains that the name of YHWH was revealed only in the time of Moses (Exod. 6:2-3) and which therefore uses only the more general terms *'elohim* and *'el shadday*.[7]

The lack of concern that the lips of a non-Israelite might contaminate the sacred name reflects a larger tendency in biblical traditon to acknowledge and honor gentiles who revere YHWH, such as Jethro (Exodus 18), Balaam (Numbers 22-24), Rahab (Joshua 2), Naaman (2 Kings 5), Job, and Cyrus (Isa. 44:24-45:10). This broadly inclusive theology demonstrates vividly the grave danger in using the term "pagan" to denote both a non-Israelite and a practitioner of a religion odious to the God of Israel: The two are not coterminous. Not every non-Israelite was thought to practice an abominated cult. Instead, biblical tradition seems to have thought that the knowledge of God, even in its most concentrated, YHWHistic form, was not necessarily the result of some miraculous incursion into nature by the deity. Rather, "YHWH is near to all who call upon, him, to all who call upon him in truth" (Ps. 145:18). Quite apart from the specific self-disclosure of God to Israel, then, the Bible assumes a natural knowledge of God available to all humanity.

The technical term for this universally available religion is *yir'at 'elohim* or *yir'at YHWH*, "the fear of God" of "the fear of the Lord," and it is associated with moral rectitude. When the Philistine king Abimelech demands to know from Abraham why he passed his wife off as his sister, the latter responds, "Because I thought there was surely no fear of God in this place and they would kill me for my wife" (Gen. 20:11). In the Hellenistic period, the term "God-fearers" (*phoboumenoi* or *sebomenoi ton theon*) came to denote a class intermediate between Jews on the one hand, and "pagans" in the derogatory sense on the other. The Noahide and the God-fearer, like the *ger toshav* of rabbinic literature (with whom they may be identical), testify to a theology that holds that the true religion is larger than the religion of the core insiders, which it includes. The convenient dichotomy of insider-outsider is too crude to accommodate the Jewish conception of the divine-human relationship.

This concept of the universal availability of God and his law remained alive and was never displaced in ancient Israel by more particularistic theologies.

Wisdom teachers were especially inclined to speak in non-national terms. The books of Proverbs, Job, and Qohelet never refer to the people of Israel, the Exodus, the Covenant of Sinai, or the gift of the Land. Instead, they address what they perceive to be the general human condition and ground moral authority not in a historical revelation — there is no evidence the authors of these books believed in a Torah of Moses — but in direct observation of the world.[8] Whereas the Pentateuchal and prophetic traditions celebrate the frightening irruption into the natural order of a passionate and unpredictable God, Wisdom literature relishes the reassuring constancy and reliability of nature and its creator. Injustice, like imbalance in nature, cannot endure, for the world-order rights itself:

> He who digs a pit will fall into it.
> And he who rolls a stone — it will roll back on him.
> (Prov. 26:27)

With its high esteem for universal truths, Wisdom theology shows an inherent tendency toward cosmopolitanism. Israelite Wisdom writers took pride in their great culture-hero King Solomon:

> Solomon's wisdom was greater than the wisdom of all the men of the East and than all the wisdom of Egypt. He was the wisest of men, wiser than Ethan the Ezrahite, Heman, Chalkol, and Darda, the sons of Mahol. His reputation spread among all the surrounding peoples. (1 Kgs. 5:10-11)

It is telling that, although the biblical historian considers Solomon's wisdom a charismatic gift from YHWH (v. 9), he also stresses the international recognition of it. Solomon's sagacity, far from being something foreign and opaque to outsiders, is actually the quintessence of something they have esteemed and pursued, with no small success. The experience of Solomon's wisdom leaves the Queen of Sheba breathless with admiration (10:5). There is no hint that she is regarded as "pagan" in the pejorative usage, and her religion does not seem to interfere with her appreciation of Solomon's perspicacity. On the contrary, he passes *her* test (10:2-3).

In all likelihood the Wisdom teachers considered the gods of the gentiles, or at least of the sagacious and ethical gentiles, as not different in kind from YHWH, the God of Israel. Perhaps they thought the different gods were really only different names for the one all-pervasive reality, which can be intuited in general human experience. It was a theology of this sort that enabled the Israelite sages to include in their proverb collections the dicta of foreign savants, such as those of the mysterious Agur ben Jake (Prov. 30:1) and Lemuel, king of Massa (Prov. 31:1-9), perhaps an Arabian emirate (cf. Gen, 25:14). The likelihood that these two men were indeed non-Israelite sages has been advanced by the discovery that Prov. 22:17-24:22 is an Israelite adaptation of the thirty-chapter "Instruction of Amen-em-opet," an Egyptian Wisdom text that probably dates from the seventh century B.C.E.[9] The biblical Wisdom teachers provide a solid precedent for the Judaization of later philosophical movements, from Platonism to existentialism. A telling way in which Jewish practice continues this openness to non-Jewish wisdom is the benediction pronounced upon seeing a gentile wise person: "Blessed are you, YHWH our God, master of the universe, who has imparted of his wisdom to flesh and blood."[10]

III. Purpose and Mystery in the Election of Israel

As the primeval history (Genesis 1-11) has it, the original unity of mankind could not endure man's increasing wickedness. From the expulsion from the Garden of Eden through the first murder and the iniquity of the generation of the Flood, the dominant note is one of curse. With the incident of the Tower of Babel, the pristine unity of humanity is shattered: persons now speak a variety of languages and dwell "over the face of the whole earth" (11:9). The familiar world of human fragmentation and diversity has been born. Its mother is rebellion, and its midwife, the curse of God.

At the beginning of the Patriarchal narratives, to our surprise, the note of curse is replaced by one of blessing: YHWH promises a Mesopotamian named Abram that he will inherit an unknown land, father a great nation, and become a byword of blessing, indeed a source of blessing to those who bless him (12:1-3). Apparently, God's high hopes for the world, continually frustrated throughout the dismal course of primeval history, are now focused on one man who will reverse the decline of a failing humanity. Unlike later rabbinic exegesis, the Torah itself offers no grounds for the selection of Abram for this awesome assignment. It makes no claim that he had earned it or that he was endowed with some genetic predisposition that made his selection rational. Instead, the Torah present the revelation to Abram as sudden and unanticipated, and his obedient response as an unalloyed act of faith. The backdrop is still universal; the relevance of his fate to the nations is announced at the outset (12:3). Yet he alone bears the promise.

The relationship of YHWH and Abraham is soon formalized as a "covenant" (Genesis 15 and 17), a treaty which the parties swear to uphold. When the parties are, as here, unequal, we speak of a "suzerainty treaty." The lord of the covenant, the suzerain, makes a pact with his subject, the vassal. In some biblical instances, as in the great covenant with all Israel concluded on Sinai, the treaty lists stipulations, in this case the *mitsvot* (commandments) of the Torah, which the suzerain enjoins upon his vassal.[11] In other cases, such as the covenant with Noah (9:1-17) and that with Abraham, the goal of the suzerain is not to secure the undivided allegiance of the vassal, but to reward his already demonstrated loyalty with a grant.[12] With Abraham, the grant includes a fiefdom, the land of Israel, as it will come to be called, and a dynasty, the people Israel, in whom kings will appear (17:6-8). In the second formulation of this covenant of grant (17:9-14), circumcision plays a central role. It is a visible "sign of the covenant" (v. 11), like the rainbow in the Noahide Covenant (9:12-17) and the Sabbath in the Sinaitic Covenant (Exod. 31:16-17).

It is significant that the Torah's promise to Abraham predates the existence of a people Israel, which indeed comes into being only as a result of YHWH's mysterious grace and the equally mysterious but edifying obedience of Abraham. By making the theology earlier than the people, the Torah underscores "the necessity of viewing the greatness of the nation in light of the greatness of her God."[13] Indeed, Israel exists only because of God's choice, and apart from God, it has no existence at all. Even those biblical traditions that date the selection of Israel from the generation of the Exodus and Sinai (e.g., Deut. 32:20; Hos. 11:1; Ezek. 20:5) rather than from Abraham assume the inseparabilty of peoplehood from theology. Israel has no profane history, only a sacred history, a history of redemption, of backsliding and return, punishment and restoration.

Ancient Near Eastern covenants, whose signatories tend to be kings, illuminate for us the Bible's account of God's covenant with the Jewish people at Sinai. The covenanted Israelites, vassals though they be, are also described in royal terms:

> And if you truly obey me and observe my covenant, you will be my special possession from among all peoples — for the whole world is mine. But you are to be my priestly kingdom and sacred nation. . . .(Exod. 19:5-6)

It has even been argued that the word translated as "kingdom" actually means "king."[14] Whether or not this is so, the language describing Israel's chosenness in the bible reflects the terms in which ancient Near Eastern kings described their relationships to their divine patrons. For example, an Egyptian text describes Hatshepsut, the female pharaoh, as "she whom he [the god] chose to protect Egypt." Mesopotamian kings were sometimes described as "the one chosen by the faithful heart of god," "the Chosen One of the gods," or "the one to whom the eyes of the gods have been directed."[15] Nebuchadrezzar I, king of Babylon in the twelfth century B.C.E., is described as "the prince beloved by Marduk — the king of the gods, Marduk commissioned him," and his younger contemporary Tiglath-Pileser I of Assyria is described as "the beloved prince, the desire of your [i.e., the gods] hearts, the exalted shepherd, whom in your faithful hearts you have called. . . ."[16]

There are other biblical instances of God's referring to those he has selected in similarly exalted language. David, chosen as king, will say to YHWH, "You are my father," and YHWH "will make him [his] firstborn son, highest of the kings of the earth" (Ps. 89:27-28; cf. 2 Sam. 7:8-16; Psalm 2). Israel, too, appears in the privileged role of YHWH's first-born son, whose desire to serve the divine father not even Pharoah may thwart (Exod. 4:22-23). This concept of the people Israel collectively as God's son grounds the demand that Israel's ways are to be visibly different from the ways of the gentiles (Deut. 14:1-2),but it also insures that God's grace will not allow even the gravest sins of Israel to provoke him to disown them (Hosea 11; Jer. 31:18-20). His paternal love elevates the covenantal relationship into something more than a *quid pro quo* deal between two self-interested politicians.

To be sure, many Christian commentators have argued that God's choice of the Jews was conditional and instrumental rather than final. "In the thought of the Old Testament, it is always election to service," wrote an eminent Christian scholar of the last generation, "and it is held to be forfeited when it has no relation to that service."[17] This interpretation of election has support in both the Near Eastern analogues and in biblical texts themselves. Hammurabi, king of Babylon in the late eighteenth century B.C.E., tells us in the prologue of his famous law code that the gods singled him out "to promote the welfare of the people. . .to cause justice to appear in the land, to destroy the wicked and the evil, that the strong might not oppress the weak. . . ."[18] In similar language, God specifies his reasons for choosing Abraham, reasons that relate not to his past, but to his and his dynasty's future: "That he might charge his children and his household after him to keep the way of YHWH by doing what is right and just, so that YHWH may bring about for Abraham what he has promised him" (Gen. 18:19). While it remains mysterious why God needs a particular individual to realize these ends and why Abraham should have been that person, and while it might seem contradictory to promote the cause of justice through a plan that favors one family over the rest of humanity, the choice itself is neither mysterious nor autonomous. It is subordinate to a larger plan encompassing goals which extend beyond the covenant relationship itself — right action and justice.

Another rationale for the selection of Israel appears in the work of the anonymous prophet of hope who wrote toward the end of the Babylonian Exile (ca. 539 B.C.E.):

> You are my witness — oracle of YHWH —
> And my servant whom I have chosen
> In order that you may know and believe in me
> And understand that I am he;
> Before me no god was formed,
> And none will be after me. (Isa. 43:10)

In this case, the choice of Israel, or at least the Israelite community in Babylonia, is subordinate to a theological purpose: to establish a beachhead of monotheism, a sodality of witnesses to the uniqueness and eternity of YHWH. This concept of a witness implies a third party who recieves the testimony, a judge or jury to be persuaded. Here, again, the horizon of particularism is universal. YHWH has commissioned Cyrus king of Persia,

> For the sake of my servant Jacob
> And of Israel my chosen one. . . .
> So that they may know from east to west
> That there is none but me:
> I am YHWH and there is no other. (Isa. 45:4, 6)

Once more, chosenness serves a larger purpose. The chosen people does not withdraw from the human family, but exercises a special office within it, an office defined by the character and will of their universal God. They are the particular witnesses — and beneficiaries — of universalism.

These texts and others like them support the claim that biblical election was instrumental, telling the ideas and values that God so esteemed that he chose one people to manifest them. But there is another side to the story. As we have seen, in much of the literature Israel's apostasy was not viewed as cancelling its original election; YHWH did not abandon it and try again with somebody else, although he once threatened to do so (Num. 14:12). Thus, although the election was on occasion articulated in terms of larger purposes, Israel's failure to serve those purposes did not necessarily terminate the election. Conversely simply serving those purposes — practicing justice and worshipping YHWH alone — did not make one an Israelite, even if it did make one a responsible citizen of the universal theocracy.

The election of Israel was only partly grounded in universals. Even after these have been taken into account, the singling-out of Israel remains a mystery:

> Not because you were more numerous than all other peoples did YHWH take a passion to you (*hashaq*) and choose you — indeed, you are the least of the peoples; but it was because YHWH loved you and kept the oath that he swore to your Patriarchs that YHWH took you out with a strong hand and redeemed you from the house of bondage, from the power of Pharaoh, king of Egypt. (Deut. 7:7-8)

Here, the choice of Israel is grounded in passion. The verb *hashaq* is also used of Shechem's tragic love for Dinah, whom he raped (Gen. 34:8), and of the feelings of an Israelite warrior upon sight of a captured woman whom he wishes to marry (Deut. 21:11). It suggests an affair of the heart, with all the irrationality and unpredictability of such things. Who can specify the reasons why he loves someone above all others of the same class, and even if he can, do those reasons ever account in full for that love? God knows what he wants to do with Israel, but why he chose this people rather than another still remains a mystery of his love.

There is, then, a duality in the Bible's concept of election. On the one hand, election is at times articulated in terms of larger purposes that it is to serve, and, of necessity, those purposes extend beyond the confines of the chosen people. On the other hand, God bears with Israel even when it fails in its mission. The purposes do not override the chosenness, and chosenness cannot be reduced merely to the commitment to certain values. The specialness of Israel is neither altogether self-sufficient nor altogether instrumental. Should the Israelites imagine that their election is totally self-sufficient, they are reminded that their exodus is not unique (Amos 9:7) and that their election is totally instrumental, depending only on their own very flawed obedience, they are reminded that the Covenant insures them an undeserved second chance (e.g., Lev. 26:39-45). Election implies service, but service renews election. God's grace implies his law, but his law implies his grace. Neither takes precedence over the other; they are inextricable.

For Jews in the post-Enlightenment West, where ideas of human equality and democratic government hold sway, there is a temptation to stress the instrumental dimension of Jewish chosenness and to deny or ignore the self-sufficient dimension. We are sometimes told that the "chosen people" means the "choosing people," as if passive and active participles were not opposite in meaning. Judaism is presented as a commitment to some rather amorphous "Jewish values", which, on inspection, turn out to be *universal* values, in which Jews and gentiles alike ought to believe. Covenant, if it is mentioned at all, appears only as the basis of a warm, meaningful community life. The fact that the Covenant distinguishes sharply between insiders and outsiders — although both are God's — is ignored.

In large measure, such attitudes are dictated by the exigencies of living as a minority in a mixed society with a high degree of openness. It is simply not prudent to affirm a distinctiveness of ultimate significance based on heredity, and what is not prudent to express publicly often loses credibility, becoming peripheral or taboo even in private discourse. In addition, the contemporary theology in question represents a cognitive surrender to a Kantian theory of ethics in which morality entails universalizability: if the behavior cannot be advocated for everyone, it cannot be moral. On Kantian principles, Jewish ethics — a norm for one group only — is a contradiction in terms.[20] Hence the common substitution of ethics for Torah. "Ethics," writes Michael Wyschogrod, "is the Judaism of the assimilated."[21]

Despite the centrality of ethics to Judaism and despite the very real universalizing aspects of biblical thought, intellectual honesty obliges us to acknowledge that the covenant-community is distinct from the universal moral law. The Israelite may eat no carrion, since he is a member of the "sacred people." The foreigner, however, may, and in Deuteronomic law (Deut. 14:21), he incurs no guilt by doing so.[22] In the Sabbatical year one Israelite is not to dun another, but he may dun a foreigner (15:3), just as an Israelite may take no interest from another, but may take it from an outsider (23:20-21).

What is the basis for such discrimination? In some instances, these laws are based on Israel's sacrality, which must be guarded from pollution, and are of the same character as those that protect the priesthood. The Book of Ezekiel, for example (44:31), forbids priests (*kohanim*) any meat which is carrion or the result of tearing by beasts. This law, which may not know of the Pentateuchal extension of prohibition to *all* Israel,[23] derives from the consecration of priesthood, and it is reasonable that the people Israel, themselves a "priestly kingdom" (Exod. 19:6), should have fallen under some of the same protections. On the other hand, the prohibition on interest-taking from a fellow Israelite probably derives from the covenant theology and its concept of the special solidarity of the covenantal community. Israelites relate to each other as fellow vassals of the same liege lord; they relate to outsiders differently. "With my friend you shall be friend, and with my enemy you shall be enemy," announced a Hittite suzerain to his vassal.[24] In Israel, friendship involved the right to free loans. "You shall love your neighbor as yourself; I am YHWH," announces one of the most memorable verses in the Torah (Lev. 19:18). But the context makes clear that the "neighbor" is one's "brother," a fellow worshipper of YHWH.[25]

There is a healthy pluralism inherent in these laws which avoids applying the same norms to all families and nations, as if familial and national indentities were insignificant. But the fact remains that Judaism and egalitarianism are in contradiction and that the universalistic thrust of modern, democratic societies undermines all particularisms, especially those based on the claim of historical revelation.

Even when a particular biblical norm does not distinguish insiders from outsiders, something essential is lost when the norm is described in the language of universal values rather than the language of commandments, as in the Torah itself. Commandments presuppose direct address: the king commands his subjects, the suzerain his vassal. The force of the commandment follows from the relationship in which it is embedded, in this case, the relationship of love and loyalty demonstrated to the satisfaction of all when YHWH took Israel out of Egypt to be his own. Values, however, which suggest meanings embedded in a uniform reality, presume no such relationship.

To be sure, this world of values is not altogether alien to the biblical traditions. Wisdom Literature, as we have seen, often speaks in such terms and, unlike the Torah, it does not ground ethics in the particularistic traditions of Exodus and Sinai. Even in the Torah itself, the larger meaning is sometimes noted (e.g., Exod. 23:25-26); not every commandment is a mysterious ukase incomprehensible to those upon whom it is enjoined. There is, in short, ample warrant in the biblical tradition for discourse in the language of values, and in contemporary America, where claims of revelation are generally considered illicit in public discourse,[26] this resort to the language of values is a necessity for the participation of religious Jews.

Nonetheless, we must not lose sight of the limitation that the structure of Judaism places upon such language. Unchecked, the tendency to recast commandments (*mitsvot*) as values renders the very existence of the Jews superfluous. Cut loose from their convenantal matrix, the commandments cease to bind those who observe them to the God of Abraham, Isaac, and Jacob. Thus, although the prerequisites of public discourse are not to be slighted, Jews must guard against importing those extramural priorities into the discourse that takes place within the community of faith, where a dialectical usage of the language of commandments and the language of values is appropriate. Neither vocabulary should be allowed to vanquish the other. Commandments and values are distinct but related.

IV. Judaism for the Gentiles

We have seen that one possible definition of a universalistic religion is a religion that accepts converts. On this issue, there seems to have been some ambiguity and significant evolution in biblical thought.

Some texts suggest that foreigners could indeed be integrated into Israel. One thinks, for example, of the "mixed multitude" (*'erev rav*) that went out of Egypt with the Israelites (Exod. 12:38). Rashi, the great medieval commentator, is perhaps correct in glossing this as a "mixture of converts from various nations" (although rabbinic definitions of Jewishness and conversion must not be anachronistically retrojected into the biblical period). A more explicit case is that of Ruth, whose moving declaration to Naomi ("Your people will be my people/And your God will be my God," 1:16) may echo some sort of liturgy of naturalization.

Even if this is so, the degree of integration of a foreigner into ancient Israel remains shrouded in obscurity. Note that even after her "naturalization," Ruth is still "Ruth the Moabite" (Ruth 4:5), and not the "Israelite." And while texts that exclude some groups altogether and admit others only after two generations imply the acceptability of those not so designated (Deut. 23:4, 8-9), Ezra and Nehemiah, in demanding the dissolution of all intermarriages, seem not to have known of any possibility of conversion for the foreign wives (Ezra 9-10; Neh. 13:23-31). Also, whereas biblical law insists that "the alien (*ger*) shall be to you like one of your citizens" (e.g., Lev. 19:34),[27] the very same equalizing law provides oblique evidence for the survival of his alien identity. In short, like the dichotomy of insider-outsider, the dichotomy between a religon that accepts converts and one that does not is too simplistic to accommodate the complex and shifting realities of biblical Israel.[28]

Whatever the precise status of the "foreigner" after his "conversion," it is clear that especially after the Babylonian Exile (sixth century B.C.E.), we hear much about a class of people who wished to attach themselves (*nilvah*) to Israel, e.g.,

> Happy is the man who does this,
> The person who holds fast to it:
> Who observes the sabbath and does not profane it,
> Who guards his hand so that it does no evil.
>
> Let not the foreigner say,
> Who has attached himself to YHWH:
> "YHWH will keep me apart from his people."
>
> . . . As for the foreigners who attach themselves to YHWH,
> To minister for him and to love the name of YHWH,
> And to become his servants,
> All who observe the Sabbath and do not profane it,
> And hold tightly to my Covenant —
>
> These I shall bring to my sacred mountain,
> And to them I shall give joy in my House of Prayer.
> Their whole-offerings and their sacrifices
> Shall find acceptance on my altar,
> For my Temple shall be called,
> "A House of Prayer for All Peoples."

Oracle of the Lord YHWH,
Who gathers the dispersed of Israel:
I will gather more to those already gathered.
(Isa. 56:2-3, 6-8)[29]

One should guard against the assumption that this text indicates the absorption of gentiles into Israel, as became possible in a later stage of Jewish history. The text does not imply naturalization — the foreigner may well remain just that — but it does endorse the acceptability of a gentile's participation in the cult of the God of Israel in Jerusalem, provided that he, in turn, accepts the Covenant. Here the sign of the Covenant is the Sabbath, which functions as the *conditio sine qua non* for cultic participation, like circumcision in some Pentateuchal texts (e.g., Exod. 12:48-49).

Whether the oracle excerpted above anticipates the full absorption of the foreigner into Israel or not, it certainly envisions an international community of YHWHists centered upon the YHWH-Temple in Jerusalem. Another oracle from the same collection goes further, envisioning foreigners serving as priests (*kohanim*) and Levites (*leviyim*), previously hereditary offices (Isa. 66:18-21). Here, as in the previously quoted passage, the new Exodus, the return of Israel from its Babylonian dispersion, attracts the attention of the gentiles and converts them to the worship of YHWH in his holy city and through his particular liturgy. Retrospectively, the image recalls the "mixed multitude" that went out of Egypt with Israel (Exod. 12:38). Prospectively, it anticipates the saying of the Talmudic authority Rabbi Elazar that "The Holy One (blessed be he) dispersed Israel into exile among the nations only so that converts may be added to them."[30]

The fact that so much of late biblical eschatology envisions the reorientation of the nations toward YHWH is highly significant.[31] It suggests something like a restoration of the situation of the primeval history (Genesis 1-11), in which humanity was united, monotheistic, and YHWHistic. History has come full circle, except that Israel does not disappear into an undifferentiated humanity. Rather, it and the nations survive, only now centered upon the service of YHWH, the universal creator, king, and redeemer, in his cosmic capital, Jerusalem. Israelite particularism is not destined to disappear. It is destined to reach its universal horizon.

In post-biblical Judaism, it was certainly licit for a gentile to be absorbed completely into the people Israel without the retention of his foreign origin. A Greek who became a Jew was no longer, in *any* sense, a Greek; he was ethnically and religiously Jewish. It is this radical understanding of conversion that made possible the Talmudic discussion of whether a convert commits incest if he marries a close relative once the latter has also converted.[32] The question could arise only because of a presumption that conversion has created a new person who is now part of a new family, the biological family of Israel, and is no longer related to his blood relatives. So zealous were the rabbis to protect converts from discrimination that quite early they enunciated the ruling that a Jew may not say to a convert, "Remember your former ancestors," a remark that in their mind constituted the "oppression of the stranger" forbidden in Exodus 22:20.[13]

Some, following in the footsteps of the inspiring early twentieth-century theologian Franz Rosenzweig, have described Christianity as the rays that shoot out into the dark night of "paganism" from the fiery star that is Judaism: Christianity is Judaism for the gentiles.[14] Be they right or wrong, they have surely obscured the essential fact that Judaism itself can also be Judaism for the gentiles.

V. Election and Equality

The early Christian Church claimed that it represented the universalistic eschatological fulfillment of biblical prophecy. According to this view, Judaism is to Christianity as exclusiveness is to inclusiveness, closedness to openness, particularism to universalism, or, not to put too fine an edge on the matter in this post-Enlightenment era, as bad is to good. The often cited prooftext for this assertion comes from an early letter of the apostle Paul:

> You are all sons of God through faith in Christ Jesus. As many of you as have been baptized into Christ have put on Christ as a garment. There is neither Jew nor Greek, neither slave nor freeman, neither male nor female. You are all one in Christ Jesus. If you are Christ's, then you are the seed of Abraham, and so heirs according to the promise. (Gal. 3:26-29)

In Paul's thinking, the way a person, Jew or gentile, falls heir to the Abrahamic promise is not, as it was for the rabbis, through birth or acceptance of the Torah, but through the pneumatic experience of baptism, which effects a spiritual transformation. Birth as a Jew and observance of the *mitsvot* are insufficient: it is faith that makes one an Israelite. Faithless Jews have lost the status of Abraham's offspring. They are like Ishmael, rejected in favor of Isaac, and like Esau, born of Isaac yet mysteriously rejected by God in favor of his brother Jacob.[15] Jews are branches mysteriously lopped off the tree to make room for the gentiles graciously being grafted on through faith in Christ.[16]

The community that Paul envisions in Galatians is indeed one that has abolished fundamental Jewish distinctions. But Paul's thinking is hardly universalistic. He does not affirm the irrelevance of Israelite identity, but only the uniqueness of faith and baptism as the means of access to it. Whether one is heir to Abraham's promise still means everything to Paul; although he specifies a different rite of passage from that of the rabbis, like them, he still assumes that whether one is in Israel or not is of supreme importance. He says that there is neither Jew nor Greek among those *in Christ* and that whether one is circumcized or not is of no account *in Christ.*[17] But he does not say, his theology does not allow him or any other Christian to say, that whether one is "in

Christ" or not is inconsequential and that whether one is *baptized* or not is of no account. Only if he said these things could he be termed a universalist in a sense in which the rabbis were not.

In point of fact, both Judaism and Christianity, to the extent that they are true to their respective foundational literatures, must continue to affirm the essential dichotomy between insiders and outsiders, even as they mitigate and complicate the dichotomy in various ways. The only difference is that the majoritarian character of Western Christianity tempts Christians to imagine that their religion is universal, whereas minority groups are not similarly tempted. But this might change. In a shrinking and often secularizing world, Christians will become increasingly aware of their own particularism and culture-conditionedness. Undoubtedly, many of them will continue to aspire to Christianize the globe; many will continue to adhere to an exclusivism as extreme as any in all of Judaism and more extreme than most, the exclusivism that affirms, in the words of the Jesus of Johannine tradition, "No one comes to the father except through me."[18] Nevertheless, the naive and unreflective contrast between a closed, ethnocentric Judaism and an open universal Christianity is likely to appear increasingly incredible.

Indeed, both Jewish and Christian identity are threatened by an egalitarian theory of justice that is popular in contemporary America. This theory identifies justice not, as in the older liberalism, with equality before the law of the pluralistic state, but, increasingly, with equality of condition: inequities are seen as *ipso facto* proof of iniquities, and distinctive roles are seen as inherently oppressive, unless they are freely chosen (in which case they cease to be distinctive roles and become "lifestyles"). Discrimination becomes the gravest of sins. (One sometimes suspects that in some people's ethics it is the *only* sin left.)

Neither Judaism nor Christianity can accede *in toto* to an egalitarian theory of justice without undermining its own basis of existence, since, as we have seen, neither community advocates a natural and undifferentiated humanity, even one with commendable values. Rather, each community claims to be Israel and to give its members a unique and otherwise unavailable opportunity for participation in divine sonship. Neither Judaism nor Christianity can fully endorse an ethic of voluntarism in which obligations and roles are always freely chosen and can be resigned at will. Indeed, both communities call for a freely given assent to an identity not devised or chosen by persons, but conferred graciously by a mysterious deity, and both refuse to recognize conversion to another identity, religious or secular.[19] In the Bible, one sees this curious simultaneous affirmation of choice and fate in Joshua's covenant ceremony at Shechem. In one breath he offers Israel the choice of which god(s) to serve, and then in the next breath avers that if they choose any other than YHWH, YHWH will annihilate them (Josh. 24:15, 20). Whether we Jews accept the *mitsvot* or not is our choice. But if we choose not to do so, we choose death (Deut. 30:15-20).

Judaism cannot survive the obliteration of the distinction between Jew and gentile (unless or until the nations convert to Judaism). Any theory of justice that disparages accidents of birth and fated roles automatically disparages Judaism. We have seen that the Bible offers impressive resources for a doctrine of human equality and that Talmud and midrash continue this stream of thought, endorsing a model of peoplehood that is non-racial and non-genetic, yet familial and earthly. But we have also seen that our sacred literature legitimates and even mandates certain forms of inequality. Modern Jews, especially in the West, have been enthusiastic advocates of equality, in part because of our tradition, in part because a persecuted group stands to gain from equalization. But we must not lose sight of the essential distinction between the idea of *civic equality* and a thorough-going *egalitarianism* that undermines Jewish existence itself. The current tendency to identify equality with justice poses both a theoretical and a practical challenge to Judaism that we must not shrink from confronting.

VI. Can Theology Be Secularized?

Our discussion of universalism and particularism in the Bible has sought to demonstrate the inadequacy of either term in dealing with the subtle, nuanced, and shifting biblical world view. On the one hand, the universality of God and of his realm are generally assumed. On the other, a single undifferentiated humanity is not assumed, except occasionally in primordial times and in some of the Wisdom Literature. The fractured unity of primeval humanity is to be restored in the reorientation of the nations toward YHWH enthroned in Jerusalem. Particularism is, on the one hand, very evident in the central concept of covenant: Israel is God's special possession, his first-born son, who is assigned special obligations, special privileges, and a special destiny. Yet Israel exists only by the will and grace of God, and is constituted for divine service.

Can this world view, assembled synchronically out of the varying materials in Scripture, survive the demise of its theological matrix? I think not. We have already noted that when commandments are recast in the language of values, the effect is to undermine subtly and usually unintentionally the very basis of Jewish existence. Here, a convenient universalism is purchased at the price of an inconvenient and undemocratic particularism.

Ironically, secularization can also result in the opposite extreme, an exaggerated particularism purchased at the cost of the universal dimension of Judaism. I am thinking, for example, of the currently common habit of stressing Jewish survival as a goal in its own right. On occasion, we even hear Judaism itself commended on the grounds that it contributes to Jewish survival: "Keep kosher so that your children won't intermarry." Instead of Israel's existing for the service of God, God exists for the service of Israel. At its worst, the absolutization of Jewish survival leads to the denial of ethical constraints of a Jewry in danger. And since Jewry is usually in danger, this grants the Jews a moral *carte blanche* — quite the reverse of the biblical intent. If "ethics is the Judaism of the assimilated,"[40] then nationalism is the Judaism of the secularized.

Nothing is more delicate than the interplay of universalism and particularism in traditional Jewish theology. Take away the theology, and the interplay disappears or mutates. Observance is precious, but observance alone cannot ensure a Jew that it is the theology, rather than one of its modern derivatives, that is most active in his or her life, There is no substitute for theologically sophisticated scrutiny of the sacred sources.

Notes

1. See Alexander Heidel, *The Babylonian Genesis* (2nd ed.; Chicago: University of Chicago, 1951), p. 48.
2. See H.W.F. Saggs, *The Encounter with the Divine in Mesopotamia and Israel* (London: University of London/Athlone, 1978), pp. 30-63.
3. See Moshe Weinfeld, "Sabbath, Temple, and the Enthronement of the Lord - The Problem of the Sitz im Leben in Genesis 1:1-2:3," in *Mélanges bibliques et orientaux en l'honneur de M. Henri Cazelles* (ed. A. Caquot and M. Delcor; Alter Orient und Altes Testament 212; Kevalaer: Butzon and Bercker; Neukirchen-Vluyn: Neukirchener, 1981), pp. 501-512.
4. On this, see Mircea Eliade, *Myth and Reality* (New York and Evanston: Harper and Row, 1963), pp. 21-38.
5. Carroll Stuhlmueller, "The Foundations for Mission in the Old Testament," in *Biblical Foundations for Mission* (ed. Donald Senior and Stuhlmueller; Maryknoll, NY: Orbis, 1983), p. 11. Stuhlmueller notes especially Ezek. 16:3.
6. See, e.g., *b.Sanh.* 65a.
7. Conventionally, the proper name of the God of Israel, YHWH is translated "the Lord," whereas the word *'elohim* is translated "God." For a convenient presentation of the hypothesis that underlies the source-critical distinctions, see E.A. Speiser, *Genesis* (Anchor Bible 1; Garden City, NY: Doubleday, 1964), pp. xxii-xliii.
8. See John J. Collins, "The Biblical Precedent for Natural Theology," *Journal of the American Academy of Religion* 45/1 Supplement (1977), pp. 35-67.
9. See *Ancient Near Eastern Texts Relating to the Old Testament* (3rd ed.; ed. James B. Pritchard; Princeton: Princeton University Press, 1969), pp. 421-425. On Wisdom Literature in general, see Joseph Blenkinsopp, *Wisdom and Law in the Old Testament The Ordering of Life in Early Judaism* (Oxford Bible Series; New York: Oxford University Press, 1983).
10. Cf. *b.Ber.* 58a, where the form is "to his creatures."
11. On covenant, see Delbert R. Hillers, *Covenant: The History of a Biblical Idea* (Seminars in the History of Ideas; Baltimore: Johns Hopkins, 1969); and Jon D. Levenson, *Sinai and Zion: an Entry into the Jewish Bible* (New Voices in Biblical Studies; Minneapolis: Winston Seabury, 1985), pp. 23-86.
12. See Moshe Weinfeld, "The Covenant of Grant in the Old Testament and in the Ancient New East," *Journal of the American Oriental Society* 90 (1970), pp. 184-205; and Jon D. Levenson, "On the Promise of the Rechabites," *Catholic Biblical Quarterly* 38 (1976), pp. 508-514.
13. Horst Seebass, "bachar," *Theological Dictionary of the Old Testament* (ed. G. Johannes Botterweck and Helmer Ringgren; Grand Rapids: Eerdmans, 1975), vol. 2, p. 84.
14. William L. Moran, "A Kingdon of Priests," in *The Bible in Current Catholic Thought* (St. Mary's Theological Studies 1; ed. John L. McKenzie; New York: Herder and Herder, 1962), pp. 7-20. But note that Moran considers the king in question to be the priesthood collectively.

15. Jan Bergman and Helmer Ringgren, "bachar" (see n. 13), pp. 73-74.
16. J.M. Powis Smith, "The Chosen People," *American Journal of Semitic Languages and Literatures* 45 (1929), pp. 74-75.
17. H.H. Rowley, *The Biblical Idea of Election* (London: Lutterworth, 1950), p. 94.
18. *Ancient Near Eastern Texts* (see n. 9), p. 164. Cf. Ps. 72:1-4, 12-14.
19. On Amos' putative universalism, see Harry M. Orlinsky, "Nationalism-Universalism and Internationalism in Ancient Israel," in *Translating and Understanding the Old Testament: Essays in Honor of Herbert Gordon May* (ed. Harry Thomas Frank and William L. Reed; Nashville-New York: Abingdon, 1970), pp. 211-212.
20. On some implications of Kant for Judaism, see Emil L. Fackenheim, "The Revealed Morality of Judaism and Modern Thought: A Confrontation with Kant," in *Rediscovering Judaism* (ed. Arnold Wolf; Chicago: Quadrangle, 1965), pp. 51-76, reprinted in Fackenheim, *Quest for Past and Future: Essays in Jewish Theology* (Boston: Beacon, 1968), pp. 204-228 and in *Contemporary Jewish Ethics* (ed. Menachem Marc Kellner; New York: Sanhedrin, 1978), pp. 61-83. In the last book, see also Norbert Samuelson, "Revealed Morality and Modern Thought," pp. 84-99.
21. Michael Wyschogrod, *The Body of Faith: Judaism as Corporeal Election* (New York: Seabury, 1983), p. 181.
22. But cf. Lev. 17:15-16, where life in the Land seems to obligate the foreigner to observe purity prohibitions.
23. Exod. 22:30; Lev. 17:15-16, Deut. 14:21. But note Lev. 22:8, which, like Ezek. 44:31, imposes the prohibition only upon priests.
24. *Ancient Near Eastern Texts* (see n. 9), p. 204.
25. See Orlinsky, "Nationalism-Universalism," p. 210. But see also Ernst Simon, "The Neighbor (*Re'a*) Whom We Shall Love," In *Modern Jewish Ethics: Theory and Practice* (ed. Marvin Fox; Columbus: Ohio State University, 1975), pp. 29-56.
26. See Franklin I. Gamwell, "Religion and the Public Purpose," *Journal of Religion* 62 (1982), pp. 272-288.
27. This "theology of the stranger" has been astutely called an "anti-election theology" by Jeremy Cott, "The Biblical Problem of Election," *Journal of Ecumenical Studies* 21 (1984), pp. 205-207.
28. See Jacob Milgrom, "Religious Conversion and the Revolt Model for the Formation of Israel," *Journal of Biblical Literature* 101 (1982), pp. 169-176.
29. On this oracle, see further Jon D. Levenson, "The Temple and the World," *Journal of Religion* 64 (1984), pp. 291-293.
30. *b.Pes.* 87b.
31. E.g., also Zech. 8:20-23; Isa. 19:16-25. It is important to note that this reorientation often occurs after the nations experience a catastrophic judgment of YHWH (e.g., Isa. 19:16). The pattern of calamity followed by restoration was an old one in Israel. On the dynamics of universalism and particularism in post-exilic literature, see Moshe Weinfeld, "Universalism and Particularism in the Period of Exile and Restoration," (in Hebrew) *Tarbiz* 33 (1964), pp. 228-242. On the dynamic in later Judaism, as illustrated through the *'aleynu* prayer, see Eugene B. Borowitz, "The Dialectic of Jewish Particularity," *Journal of Ecumenical Studies* 8 (1971), pp. 560-574.
32. E.g., *b.Yeb.* 22a. See also *Mishneh Torah*, *Hilkhot 'Issurey Bi'ah* 14:10-16.
33. M. *B. Metz.* 4:10 (b. *B. Metz.* 58b). See also *Shulkhan Arukh*, *Hoshen Hammishpat* 228:2. This is not, of course, to claim that the full accceptance of converts was (or is) a consistent social reality or that resistance to converts and suspicion of them is not to be found in rabbinic sources (note that a *kohen* may not marry a convert). All I claim is that powerful halakhic and and aggadic currents oppose and mitigate this resistance and suspicion.

34. See Franz Rosenzweig, *The Star of Redemption* (New York: Holt, Reinhart, and Winston, 1970), pp. 336-379. This is a translation of the second German edition (1930). For a thorough discussion, see John T. Pawlikowski, *Christ in the Light of the Christian-Jewish Dialogue* (Studies in Judaism and Christianity; A stimulus Book; New York: Paulist, 1982), pp. 8-35.
35. Rom. 9:6-13.
36. Rom 11:13-18. But Paul's ambivalence does not allow us to make systematic sense of his letters. Note his implication of the continued election of the Jews in passages like Rom. 11:1-6, 19-24.
37. Gal. 3:26-29 and 5:6. For a hard-headed assessment of Paul's actual social views, see G.E.M. de Ste. Croix, *The Class Struggle in the Ancient Greek World* (Ithaca, N.Y.: Cornell University, 1981), pp. 103-111; 418-425.
38. John 14:6.
39. Similar statements could be made of Islam.
40. See n. 21.

VI

People and Covenant

BY ROLF RENDTORFF

I

This paper deals with one main topic in Christian-Jewish relations. If we speak on relations, at least two parties are involved. Therefore, whatever we will think and say with regard to Christian-Jewish relations, on the one hand will affect our view of Judaism or the Jewish people, but on the other hand our own self-definition as Christians as well.

One of the most crucial points where this double aspect of the problem becomes quite obvious is the definition of the meaning of the biblical term "people of God" or "God's people." Christians of previous generations had no problems with this definition because for them it has been evident that after Christ there was only one people of God, namely the Christian church. Whatever had been said in biblical texts about God's people and the like, including the name of Israel, only has been understood as referring to the church.

There could be different approaches to this problem. The easiest and least aggressive one would be just to ignore the mere existence of a Jewish people after Christ. It was, and I believe still is, a usual way, to speak about certain biblical traditions in the past tense, e.g., "The Jews used to celebrate Passover this and that way." I have to confess that this was the manner I myself have been taught about Jews and Judaism during my studies forty years ago. And for a long time I did not feel the need to question this attitude. In such a concept actually no conflict is felt between church and Israel, because the church is simply identified with the biblical Israel and seemingly there is no rivalry with any other claim.

But unfortunately, this concept of simply ignoring the Jews had not been dominant during the history of Christianity. On the contrary, the Christian main stream thinking saw the replacement of Israel by the church as a demonstration of God's punishment over the unfaithful Jewish people. One basic paper in this field, the "Ecumenical Considerations on Jewish-Christian Dialogue" by the World Council of Churches[1], put it this way:

> A classical Christian tradition sees the Church replacing Israel as God's people, and the destruction of the second temple of Jerusalem as a warrant for this claim. The covenant of God with the people of Israel was only a preparation for the coming of Christ, after which it was abrogated. (2.3).

Here the interrelation between those two aspects has been expressed clearly: The church defines itself as having replaced Israel as God's people. But to make this possible, the Jewish people has to be displaced from its original biblical stand. The Christian self-definition includes the devaluation of the Jewish people, and even the declaration of its non-existence, because now the church stands at the place that had been held by Israel before.

Still another aspect is referred to by this quotation, namely the abrogation of the covenant. This idea still goes beyond that of replacement, because here God's covenant with Israel, which is one of the central issues of the Old Testament, has been declared invalid. I do not intend in the framework of this paper to explain the "fateful consequences" of such a theological perspective as the Ecumenical Considerations do in the following paragraph (2.4). Today more and more Christians are aware of it. My point rather is what consequences a changing approach to this question will have.

II

Let me start with another important paper published earlier by the World Council of Churches, the so-called "Bristol Reports."[2] In my view, it was the first time that a changing approach to this problem had been envisaged and that the possible consequences had been discussed in the framework of Christian churches. The Bristol Report says:

> Some are convinced that, despite the elements of continuity that admittedly exist between present day Jews and Israel, to speak of the continued election of the Jewish people alongside the Church is inadmissible. It is the Church alone, they say, that is theologically speaking, the continuation of Israel as the people of God, to which now all nations belong. Election and vocation are solely in Christ, and are to be grasped in faith . . . .

> Others of us are of the opinion that it is not enough merely to assert some kind of continuity between the present-day Jews — whether religious or not — and ancient Israel, but that they actually are still Israel, i.e., that they still are God's elect people. These would stress that after Christ the one people of God is broken asunder, one part being the Church which accepts Christ, the other part Israel outside the Church, which rejects him, but which even in this rejection remains in a special sense beloved by God.

I want to add a quotation from the Ecumenical Considerations which had been published 15 years later:

> The relationship between the two communities, both worshipping the God of Abraham, Isaac and Jacob, is a given historical fact, but how it is to be understood theologically is a matter of internal discussion among Christians . . . (2.10).

If we compare the two quotations, we will realize two different aspects. On the one hand, the relationship of the two communities of faith is now taken as "a given historical fact." The thesis of the church's replacing Israel had been explicitly rejected. But on the other hand, no theological solution seems to be available for the problem raised by the existence of the Jewish people alongside the church, while its election had not been abrogated. Here it becomes quite clear what I have mentioned at the beginning: that the question of Christian-Jewish relations necessarily involves the question of Christian self-definition. In a sense one could say, that the problem becomes more complicated as soon as the continuous election of the Jewish people is accepted.

If we look at the terminology, in many documents we will find the expressions "God's people" and "covenant" to be used in an alternative and almost identical sense. Let me give one more example, this time taken from a statement by the Presbyterian Church of the USA from 1987[1]:

> We affirm that the church, elected in Jesus Christ, has been engrafted into the people of God established by the covenant with Abraham, Isaac, and Jacob. Therefore, Christians have not replaced Jews.

In this conception, the covenant is the basis of the people of God, and the church has been engrafted into this covenantal people.

III

Before taking up this line, I want to make a few remarks to the use and misuse of biblical language with regard to our topic. There is a common use of certain contrasting expressions, such as the church being the "new Israel" as opposed to the old one, or the church being the 'Ισραηλ κατα πνευμα as opposed to the 'Ισραηλ κατα σαρκα. I believe that meanwhile many will have realized that there is no New Testament evidence for such a language. Neither the expression "new Israel" nor 'Ισραηλ κατα πυευμα do occur in the New Testament. Only one time we find the expression 'Ισραηλ του θεου

(Gal 6:16), but it is uncertain to whom it refers; another time the expression 'Ισραηλ κατα σαρκα appears (1Cor 10:18), but rather meaning the "historical Israel" without negative overtones.

As a matter of fact, Paul uses the name "Israel" exclusively for the Jewish people, even emphasizing "They are Israelites" (Rom 9:4), and everything what is said about Israel in the Bible (i.e. our Old Testament) is still valid for them. The same is true for the expression λαος του θεου which is mainly used for Israel.

Thus, a re-examination of New Testament terminology shows that later Christian tradition has developed a theology of replacement or substitution which is not in accordance with the New Testament. Perhaps this is not by itself an argument for the judgement of the legitimacy of illegitimacy of a certain theological development. But nevertheless, the accordance or discord of certain Christian theological conceptions with the New Testament should not be veiled, but clearly stated, and in the case of discord also should be justified vis-a-vis the New Testament. And because particularly Paul is often quoted as a witness to the traditional Christian prejudices towards the Jewish people, it should be made clear that this is impossible and illegitimate.

IV

So far, I have briefly discussed certain aspects of the dogmatic tradition as well as some exegetical questions. Now I want to add a third dimension to the problem, namely that of the historical situation at the time of the emergence of Christianity. In traditional Christian thinking, from the outset there had been an opposition between Judaism and Christianity, and even Jesus' teaching and preaching usually has been viewed and depicted as contradicting the contemporary Jewish thinking and belief.

This view has been fundamentally revised during the last few decades. Again, the Bristol Report was the first to state the fact that Christianity emerged *within* Judaism:

> The first community of Christians were Jews who had accepted Jesus as the Christ. They continued to belong to the Jewish communities and the relationship between them and their fellow-Jews was close, notwithstanding the tension that existed between them ...

Since then, many documents have stated this fact and even have taken it as a starting point for their own considerations on the relations between Jews and Christians.

At the beginning, the Christian community was part of the Jewish community and of the Jewish people. I think it would be useful to stay at this point for a while. How could the relations between Jews and Christians be defined at this stage? There was only one Jewish people which according to the traditions written down in its Holy Scriptures, defined itself as the people of God. In the middle of this people, there was a group of Jews who believed that one of the main expectations and hopes of the Jewish people, namely the coming of the Messiah, had become true. As far as we can see from the New Testament, there was no discussion between this minority and the rest of the Jews about the question of being Israel or the people of God. All of them belonged to Israel, notwithstanding their disagreement on the question of Jesus' being the Messiah or not.

Obviously, one of the reasons why they did not feel the need to discuss this problem was the eschatological tension in which all of them lived, the group of believers in Jesus as the Messiah even more than the rest. The only relevant question was: Who will be saved when the end comes? Who will be among those that will enter the kingdom of God when it appears? This was not a matter of definition, and not a theoretical question at all.

It was a fundamental change of the situation when an increasing number of Gentiles began to join the Jewish-Christian congregations outside the land of Israel. From that time on, no longer all Christians were members of the Jewish people. By that a new question arose, namely, how to understand the promises given to Israel in the Holy Scriptures. To whom are they addressed? To the Jewish people alone? Or to the believers from non-Jewish origin as well? Or exclusively to the believers of whatever origin?

I believe it to be very important to realize at what stage of the development of the Christian community this question emerged, and why. It was because of the fact that no longer all Christians at the same time were Jews. Only from that time on the terminological distinction between Jews and Christians would make sense. And this included the before-mentioned question: Who will be the true addressee of the promises given to Israel in the Holy Scriptures. This question easily could be simplified by asking: Who is Israel? And if the answer would be given: Those who believe in Jesus Christ the Messiah, then there was only one step to the claim that the original Israel, namely the natural offspring of Abraham, did not exist any longer.

By this historical deduction I wanted to demonstrate that the question of the existence or non-existence of the original Israel as the people of God, first of all is a problem of Christian self-definition. If *we* are the true addressees of God's promises to his people, then the original people must have ceased to exist, or at least must have lost its right to claim to be God's people. This "either - or" is the basic reason for the whole debate.

The debate had begun already during Paul's lifetime. In his letter to the Christian congregation in Rome he had to discuss this problem. In chapter 9 to 11 he is answering a number of rhetorical questions which most likely are questions that had been discussed in the Rome congregation. The peak of his argumentation is the question: "I ask, then, has God rejected his people?" (Rom 11:1) Obviously, certain people in the congregation had argued that God had done this. Paul's answer is clear and unambiguous: "By no means!" It is one of the strangest elements in the Christian tradition that even Paul, as I mentioned before, usually has been taken as a witness for the doctrine of Israel's rejection, against his clear own words.

Indeed, Paul was struggling with the fact that not all Israel had acknowledged and accepted Jesus as the Messiah. For him, this was an existential problem. But nevertheless, he never would have accepted the idea that God had rejected, or ever could reject his people.

V

Traditional Christian language used to say: *We* are the people of God, not the Jews. Now, if we accept the results of rereading the New Testament, what will be the consequences? If we are saying: According to our Bible, Israel never ceased to be God's elect people — how shall we continue? Shall we say: They are the people of God, not we? Or shall we say: Both of us are the people of God? And if so, would that mean: Each of us is the — or one — people of God, or: both of us together are the one people of God?

First of all, I want to draw our attention to the shift of approach which is included in those questions. Traditionally, Christians asked whether and how there could be found a place for the Jewish people in the framework of Christian theology. Now, the problem has turned the other way round: We as Christians have to define where we ourselves come in. The Jewish people had been in existence long before the Christian community emerged in its midst. The theological consequences of this historical fact still have to be drawn. Thereby a crucial point will be that not we as Christians can claim the right to define what Judaism and the Jewish people is or should be. We can only define our own identity in relation to the Jewish people, thereby taking into account the New Testament texts as well as the Jewish self-definition.

Earlier, I quoted the Bristol Report saying, "that after Christ the one people of God is broken asunder." Since then, the idea of the one people of God is to be found in several other documents as well. But often it is added that "how (this relation) is to be understood theologically is a matter of internal discussion among Christians" (Ecumenical Considerations 2.10). Obviously, it is rather difficult to claim the expression "people of God" for both communities, the Jewish people as well as the church.

The above quoted statement by the Presbyterian Church of the USA from 1987 says, "that the church, elected in Jesus Christ, has been engrafted into the people of God established by the covenant with Abraham, Isaac, and Jacob." Here the word "engrafted" refers to Paul's picture of the olive tree (Rom 11:17ff). The tree is identified with the "people of God." But then another theological category is added, namely that of "covenant." I want to take up this line and to develop it a few steps farther.

The Synod of the Protestant Church of the Rhineland (Germany)[4] in 1980 declared:

> We believe in the permanent election of the Jewish people as the people of God and realize that through Jesus Christ the church is taken into the covenant of God with his people.

Here the two expressions "people" and "covenant" explicitly are differentiated from each other. The term "people of God" is only used for the Jewish people, and it is explicitly stated that this is the people which according to the biblical tradition had been elected by God to be his own people. It is also stated that this election is still valid. But then the next step follows: God had established a covenant with his people. This covenant now is expanded to include also the non-Jews who joined those Jews who believed that Jesus was "the one who was to come," and by their inclusion the church began to develop. This church is not part of the people of God itself, but it shares the same covenant together with the Jewish people, the people of God.

I believe this differentiation to be very helpful. It avoids the impasse to which so far the attempts have led to define "the two peoples in one," or "the one people divided into two." As Christians we have to learn that we should not use the term "people of God" as a definition of ourselves. We are not entitled to do so. But we should also understand that this is not simply a loss but that it provides us with a new way of understanding our relations to the Jewish people, and at the same time to understand our own origins better and in a more adequate way, first of all in a way that avoids any bias against the Jewish people.

Therefore for Christians the main point is to understand two things that are closely related to each other. On the one hand to realize that our own Christian origins are deeply rooted in the Jewish tradition so that we cannot define our identity without speaking about our Jewish roots. But on the other hand to understand that we are not Jews ourselves, and that means, that we are not members of the Jewish people which in biblical terms is the people of God. The bridge between these two seemingly incompatible aspects could be the biblical notion of covenant. It is one of the expressions by which in biblical language God's relationship to Israel is expressed. But at the same time it is broader so that it can include other peoples as well.

This is just a first step to try to overcome an impasse in redefining Christian identity in relation to the Jewish people. We will have to study intensively the biblical notion of covenant in both parts of our Christian Bible. In doing so, we should not restrict our examination to mere terminology like berith and διαθηκη, but to the notion or concept that is expressed by these and other related terms. One of the most important words expressing the relations of Israel and the nations God spoke to Abraham at the very beginning of his story with his people: "In you all the families of the earth shall be blessed" — or according to the JPS translation: "And all the families of the earth shall bless themselves by you" (Gen 12:3). I find it very meaningful that in the first word God spoke to the first Jew all the families of the earth are already included. We have forgotten that for a long time, but now we are beginning to rediscover it, and it is worth all efforts to work it out and to bring it to the minds of both, Christians and Jews.

Notes

1. This paper was adopted by the Executive Committee of the World Council of Churches in 1982; see A. Brockway and others, *The Theology of the Churches and the Jewish People. Statements by the World Council of Churches and its member churches. With a commentary*, Geneva 1988, p. 34-42.
2. This document was accepted by the Committee on the Church and the Jewish People of the World Council of Churches in Bristol in 1967, see ibid. p. 13-28.
3. Statement on "A Theological Understanding of the Relationship between Christians and Jews," adopted by the General Assembly of the Presbyterian Church (USA) in 1987, see ibid., p. 105-120.
4. Statement of the Synode der Evangelischen Kirche im Rheinland "Zur Erneuerung des Verhältnisses von Christen und Juden" (Towards Renovation of the Relationship of Christians and Jews), adopted in 1980, see ibid., p. 92-94.

Part II

The Way of Commemoration

VII

Do This in Memory of Me: Interreligious Reflections on Remembrance in Christianity

BY JOHN T. PAWLIKOWSKI

In the course of its nearly two millenia of existence the Christian religion has certainly given attention to the interior life of its members and explored the layered realms of mystical understanding. But by and large it has never pursued this dimension of human living to the total abandonment of its sense of being an *historical* religion. Christianity's primary identification has always been as a faith community rooted in decisive saving events which have occurred in the historical realm. Its principal sacred festivals (Christmas, Epiphany, Easter and Ascension/Pentecost) and its central liturgical celebrations (Baptism and Eucharist) are all connected to concrete events in human history whose memory has been preserved in the theology and cult of the community.

Christianity's sense of historical memory is not easily defined nor even described. It is neither simply cyclic like the ancient outlook (still preserved in many cultures) nor linear which has ruled Western consciousness since the Enlightenment. Many scholars point to the Greek word *anamnesis* which Lutheran liturgist Frank C. Senn calls virtually untranslatable into English.[1] English terms such as "memorial," "commemoration," "remembrance" tend merely to turn our attention to the past. *Anamnesis*, on the other hand, signifies far more. Somehow the person or event it brings to mind becomes present again. Senn suggests that the closest approximation might in fact be a rather awkward word "reactualization."

In trying to come to grips with this term Don E. Saliers emphasizes that in the Christian tradition remembering does not involve merely the elaboration of beliefs based on events. Rather it is seen as integral to contemporary faith expression. These are his words:

> In asking God to remember us and by invoking the Spirit to aid us in remembering who God is, we touch on the paradox of how the past becomes radically present. The forms of being called to remembrance of what has taken place between God and our stories in the past give us a future as well. This suggests that authentic biblical worship is a peculiar kind of "future present," but always grounded in the mystery and suffering of real human history.[2]

The word *anamnesis*, as used in early Christianity, was part of the vocabulary of *koine* rather than classical Greek. That means that while the word was Greek in form the mindset behind it was essentially semitic (Hebrew/Aramaic). Hence both Christian liturgical and biblical scholars who have studied the question in recent decades, and there are many, see a definite connection between the sense of remembrance in the apostolic church and its corresponding notion in Judaism. This is particularly true with respect to the role of "remembrance" in the celebration of the sacraments of Baptism and Eucharist.

The Hebraic equivalent for the Greek term *anamnesis* is the root *zkr*. The word is utilized in various places in the Hebrew Scriptures, not all of them liturgical settings. Once such use is found in Genesis 40:14 which narrates the story of Joseph while a prisoner in Egypt. Here Joseph explains the dreams of the chief baker and the chief butler. He tells the latter that his restoration to office is imminent. When this does occur, he asks that the butler "remember" him to Pharaoh so that he too should be set free. The episode ends with the remark that the butler ignored Joseph's plea, or to use the word of the text itself, he "forgot" him.

This example illustrates something of the consciousness behind the Hebrew term "to remember" (and its opposite "to forget"). They point to something far broader than good or bad memory. As used in this passage, the term *zkr* certainly connotes a linkage with the past. Joseph and the butler were imprisoned together and, while there, Joseph acted kindly toward the butler. But its primary emphasis is on what is required of the butler here and now. Recalling the past relationship serves as a potential stimulus to action in the present. Thus "remembering" is not a neutral term. Rather it places the past in the present setting, as it where, in order to prompt a person to concrete action. A similar use of the term can be found in other texts in the Hebrew Scriptures, especially 1 Samuel 25: 30-1, 39-40 and Esther 2:1.

This understanding of "remembering" contrasts significantly with the way in which we employ the term today. For the writers of the Hebrew Scriptures it is not a question of somehow re-entering past history but rather a sense that the past continues to exist in the present moment. Unfortunately, as Don Saliers notes, we have all but abandoned this biblical sense of "remembering" in contemporary Christianity to the impoverishment of our spirituality. As he puts it,

> Not to be remembered by God is a profound threat to humanity. For the biblical writers, not to be remembered has the force of death. In Isaiah 23:16 and 65:17, for example, we note that to be remembered no more by God is to be cut off from the land of living, from identity, history and thus from life itself.[3]

In this context we can understand better the force of Elie Wiesel's now famous remark that to forget the victims of the Holocaust is in fact to kill them a second time.

The general sense of "remembering" that prevailed in Hebraic consciousness also applied to the specifically religious realm. The religious use of the term appears particularly in Deuteronomy where Israel is summoned to "remember" God's saving deeds in the deliverance of the people from Egyptian captivity. (Deut 5:15; 15:15; 16:12; 24:18, 22). Here again the overriding emphasis is not on earlier historical divine deeds, but rather on the fact that these deeds demand a response from the covenantal community in their present circumstances. As Bastiaan van Iersel explains it,

> Remembering is therefore always the basis for keeping the law, the purpose of Deuteronomy. Such remembrance is therefore no turning away from the present. On the contrary, it brings the past as close as possible so that it becomes a starting point to the present, because of the consequences implied for Israel's present conduct. The same holds for the exhortation to "remember" the law which Yahweh gave to Moses (Num 15:38-40; Josh 1:13ff; Mal 3:22).[4]

The reverse of "remembering," losing sight of the divine salvific deeds, is tantamount to apostasy in the biblical perspective as we see in both Judges (8:33ff) and Isaiah (17:9-11). And when *zkr* appears in a text concerned with Israel's sinfulness, we are given a decisive example of the primacy of the present in terms on its fundamental meaning. In passages such as Hosea 8:13 which speaks of divine anger over the Israelites' involvement in the sacrifice of flesh while they neglect the other covenantal responsibilities, a situation which may lead to their return to exile in Egypt, the connection between "remember" and punishing is made quite explicit. The two terms become virtually identical. Isaiah 43:25, though it highlights divine forgiveness through the forgetting of transgressions rather than punishment through remembering, in effect makes the same point.

These various texts from the Hebrew Scriptures, and there are more, clearly strike a common chord. To remember someone or something does not remove us from the immediacy of the present. Rather the act of remembrance brings the effects of past actions and the lives of those who have gone before us into contemporary reality in a way that calls for a response from the person or community that initiates the act today.

Liturgical scholars have underlined the fact that this biblical sense of remembering lies at the heart of Jewish sacred festivals. The central celebration in the Jewish calendar, the feast of Pesach, illustrates this integral linkage. Commemorating ritually Israel's deliverance from bondage in Egypt (cf. Exod 12:1-20), its focus ultimately falls on the effect of this saving event on the celebrating community. This emphasis becomes quite evident in the Mishnaic commentary on Pesach where the text underlines the need for the present community to see itself as having been delivered from Egypt into freedom. To quote Bastiaan van Iersel once more,

> In the celebration of the Pasch, God's saving action becomes actual in word and rite each year, so that everyone who takes part in the celebration also takes part in the deliverance and redemption.[5]

Much the same holds true for the manner in which the Jewish community celebrates liturgically the Feast of the Tabernacles which recalls the Israelites' dwelling in tents at the time of the exodus from Egypt (Lev 23:33-43) as well as for the annual observance of Purim. The latter keeps alive the memory of the Israelites' experience of diaspora deliverance in the midst of persecution (Esth 9:19-28). Both celebrations aim at making the historical events a source of contemporary faith identity and action for the worshipping community.

Though my assigned responsibility in this Jewish-Christian-Islamic conference is to present the Christian approach to remembrance, it has been necessary to set the proper context for such a discussion by summarizing the Jewish biblical tradition from which it developed. Though Frank Senn quite correctly cautions against any overly facile comparisons between the Christian liturgical tradition and Jewish worship on this point,[6] it is nonetheless apparent that a close connection does exist most evidently in the Eucharist and possibly, according to some scholars, in the sacrament of Baptism as well. In addition, the celebration of Advent and Easter both revolve in a significant way around remembrance.

The Eucharistic celebration has been the Christian liturgical action where the theme of remembrance has most clearly occupied a central place since the very earliest days of church tradition. A formal anamnesis or memorial came into Eucharistic texts in connection with the inclusion of the narrative of Jesus' institution of the sacrament. In the Anaphora of Hippolytus the narrative of institution becomes the climax in a prayer of thanksgiving for the wonders of God in human history. The words of Jesus, "Do this in remembrance of me," introduce the memorial of his death and resurrection. It is interesting to note that very early Eucharistic traditions such as those in *Didache*, the *Acts of Thomas*, and the Mar Esaya text of the Anaphora of Addai and Mari which have no reference to the text of institution also lack a formal anamnesis.

While the notion of remembrance has always remained an important part of the Christian Eucharist, its meaning underwent a certain amount of change and development, especially in the Roman tradition, as the years passed. Gradually the institution text and the anamnesis come to be seen as a warrant for the church's act of oblation, rather than as the climax of salvation history's recapitulation. Because the words of institution acquired consecratory force in the Western church, associated with the trans-substantiation of the elements, medieval theologians looked upon the anamnesis-oblation to be an offering of the body and blood of Christ. This is especially evident in Eucharistic Prayer IV of the current Roman Sacramentary. This growing emphasis on the remembrance-thanksgiving linkage has led to considerable, ongoing controversy within the family of Christian denominations since the time of the Reformation.

The change in focus with respect to remembrance in the Christian Eucharistic tradition, especially in the Roman tradition, carries important consequences for the theology of the church's relationship to the Jewish people. For the more remembrance becomes tied to sacrifice rather than to the recital of the history of salvation, the more Jews disappear from the scene in terms of ongoing significance for Christian theology. This is not to say that the older Eucharistic tradition automatically guarantees a positive understanding of Christian-Jewish bonding. It does, and has, not. For it can all too easily fall into the fulfillment/displacement model that has left little theological meaning for Judaism after the Christ Event. But at least tying remembrance far more to the history of salvation rather than to sacrifice brings Jews into the picture, however much our understanding of their ongoing role requires adjustment today.

In concluding our look at remembrance and the Christian Eucharist one final point, emphasized by both liturgical and scriptural scholars, needs to be underlined. The Pauline text in 1 Corinthians (11:26) which records Jesus' command, "For as often as you eat this bread and drink the cup, you proclaim the Lord's death until he comes" clearly implies that the commemoration of the Lord's Supper constitutes a re-presentation of Jesus' death on the cross, not only in the ritual meal but also in the proclamation accompanying this rite. This is precisely what distinguishes the Eucharistic celebration from an ordinary meal. What the gathered community remembers is the death of the Lord, the divine act of redemption accomplished through the Lord Jesus, in which the partakers of the meal now share in much the same way as the Jewish people share in the Passover redemption in the Pesach meal liturgy. The emphasis is not on the transformation of the elements, but on the contemporary transformation of the people involved in the rite. If Jews and Christians were to come to a mutual understanding of their commonality in this respect in connection with remembrance this might indeed represent a genuine breakthrough in interreligious understanding despite the continued differences between them over the central remembrance event. There may also be some room here for a mutuality of understanding with the Islamic community. If so, it might be possible to recover that remarkable level of interreligious understanding that characterized Spain for a short time in the Middle Ages. Certainly if one has savored the marvels of a place like Toledo, which I have, it becomes impossible not to marvel at the breakthrough in the level of tri-faith understanding that occurred in this period even though each community remained steadfast in its distinctive theological convictions.

Certain Christian liturgical scholars such as Bastiaan van Iersel have also pointed to a somewhat less evident, but nonetheless equally real, emphasis on remembering in the texts used in the sacrament of Baptism. These texts seem to take their inspiration from the same Hebrew root *zkr* that underlies the celebration of the Eucharist in Christian worship.

Two points in particular need to be highlighted in terms of the linkage between remembering and baptism. First of all, looking at the traditional baptismal formula, "to baptize in the name of Jesus Christ" which is found in several places in Acts (e.g. 2:38; 8:16) and which seems pre-supposed in 1 Corinthians (1:13) and probably as well in Romans (6:3) and Galatians (3:27), we notice that it carries multiple meanings. In one sense the formula conveys the sense of a permanent bonding between the one baptized and him in whose name the baptism is done. But the text says something more. It also makes an important statement about the manner in which the ritual act is performed. The pronouncing of the name of Jesus Christ or the Father, Son and Holy Spirit are critical to the full meaning of the text. It is in the pronouncing of the name over the person being brought into membership in the faith community that the connection with remembering is to be found according to van Iersel:

> . . . this pronouncing is much more than a juridical or quasi-juridical action by which the baptized person is as it were formally made over and becomes the "property" of Christ. It rather calls forth that actual happening of salvation in Christ, makes present again what God has done through Jesus and saves the baptized person by bringing him out of death and darkness into the light of Christ (Eph. 5:14; cf. vv. 8 and 11; Col. 1: 12-3; 1 Peter 2:9; Heb. 6:4 and 10:32).[7]

The second point bears a relationship to the first. If the formula "to baptize in Christ" may be understood as a shortened version of "to baptize in the name of Christ," then Paul's comments in Romans (6:3) in fact become an amplification of the original baptismal injunction: "Do you not know that all of us who have been baptized into Christ Jesus were baptized into his death?" Understood in this sense it becomes apparent that Baptism, along with Eucharist, calls forth and makes present the death of Jesus. Through the ritual act the baptized person actually shares in this experience of death. And this holds not merely for Jesus' death. The remainder of the text in Romans (6:4-11) leaves little question that the newly baptized person joins Jesus in the experience of his resurrection as well. The very descent into the baptismal water and the rising out of it are seen as a ritual representation of Jesus' burial and rising: "And you were buried with him in baptism, in which you were also raised with him through faith in the working of God, who raised him from the dead." (Col 2:12).

At the baptism the presider pronounces the name of Jesus or of Father, Son and Holy Spirit over the baptized person. Through this act the newly baptized, if an adult, and the worshipping community are brought face to face with God's raising of Jesus from the dead. But this is not solely, or even primarily, historical memory devoid of any call to personal commitment on the part of those who remember. Rather it immediately assumes the status of a saving event as

Romans (6:5-11) and Colossians (2:20-3:17) make clear. Thus Jesus' resurrection becomes actual in the baptismal moment and even beyond that in the conduct of the person who now understands himself or herself as dead to sin and living for God in Christ Jesus (Rom 6:11).

van Iersel concludes his study of remembrance and its baptismal connections with the strong assertion that the sacrament must increasingly be viewed as a "memorial celebration," a commemoration in every sense of the term. This will likely necessitate in his estimation some adjustments in the manner in which baptism is celebrated in the Christian churches so that the dimension of a memorial celebration stands out far more prominently than it does at the present time.

Don Saliers also emphasizes the connection between remembering and Baptism, though in slightly different tones than van Iersel. His stress is far more on the continuing impact of the sacrament in the life of the believing member of the community. This impact is heightened in his judgment at those moments when individuals, as part of a worshipping community, *remember* their baptism in the context of liturgy. The most meaningful setting in this regard for many Christians would be the remembrance of one's baptism that is an integral part of the church's celebration of the Easter Vigil. But though the setting of remembrance may be different for Saliers and van Iersel, the fundamental significance of this act of remembering is not. For Saliers it is

> a matter of recognition of all that God has done and is yet to do in our lives. Remembering moments of great crisis, submission, and "blessed assurance" is a significant part of the community's history — as well as each believer's history and identity. But recognition of the saving mystery beyond our conscious personal experiences is also necessary. Remembering specific experiences is itself dependent upon the unfolding mystery of our life in Christ.[8]

These words of Saliers bring to the fore the very same point that van Iersel made relative to the original experience of the sacrament of Baptism. Salvific participation in the process of redemption associated with the Christ Event is the central feature of the act of remembrance.

Salier's comments also point to another dimension of remembrance which van Iersel develops as well at some length. It is the inherent link between remembrance and participation in the life and memory of a community. For Saliers recognition of this linkage lies at the heart of authentic Christian spirituality. Through Baptism and through the periodic ritual remembrance of the original sacrament the Christian believer is gradually made new or whole in Christ. But he or she likewise becomes adopted heir of the tradition of divine promises since the beginning of creation which have been preserved in the collective memory of the covenanted community. For Saliers, and this is a most important perspective given the dialogical nature of our discussion, the Christian believer is engrafted into the history of Israel and "thus must come to terms with a history not ours. We must grow into our inheritance."[9]

As Saliers understands it, Baptism is not merely an entry into the salvific process inaugurated by Christ. It is rather participation in a much longer history of a people with whom God had dwelt. Christ is the specific point of admission to that history for the non-Jew. This vision of Saliers has marked similarities to the theological outlook on the Church's relationship to the Jewish people proposed by such contemporary theologians as Paul van Buren.[10]

van Iersel chooses to frame his discussion of the communal dimension of remembrance in terms of "the corporative person" which he admits is an exceptionally cumbersome phrase. The notion has its basis in the Hebrew Scriptures. In the New Testament its principal occurrence is to be found in Romans, especially in the text about Adam and Christ (5:12-21).

Paul commences his discussion in this section of the letter by forging a link between the dying and rising Christ and those who descend and arise from the baptismal waters. One notes a genuine sense of identification between them in the Pauline view: "Do you not know that all of us have been baptized into Christ Jesus were baptized into his death? We were buried therefore with him by baptism into death, so that as Christ was raised from the dead by the glory of the Father, we too might walk in newness of life. For if we have been united with him in a death like his, we will certainly be united with him in a resurrection like his. We know that our old self was crucified with him so that the sinful body might be destroyed, and we might no longer be enslaved to sin .... But if we have died with Christ, we believe that we shall also live with him." (Rom 6:3-8)

The remarkable sense of unity that Paul puts forward in this text can only be understood against the backdrop of the prevailing notion of a "corporative person." The identity with Christ resulting from the baptismal experience is not merely an individual reality. Rather it is an experience in and through the community. Because those baptized partake in the corporative personality of Christ, they will also partake in the "corporative person" to whom Christ belongs, and share therefore in the original promises made to Abraham. This particular sense of linkage to Abraham envisaged by Paul as part of the total experience of baptism may indeed prove a fruitful starting point for a discussion of the bonds between the three faith communities present at this conference. The Abrahamic dimension is also the reason why Paul feels himself on target in comparing baptism with circumcision: "In him also you were circumcised," not through the specific ritual act of the Jewish tradition, but through that circumcision of Christ which is baptism. "And you were buried with him in baptism, in which you were also raised with him through faith in the working of God, who raised him from the dead." (Col 2:11)

The notion of the "corporative person" connects up in Pauline literature with the idea of "one body." This allows Paul to extend his perspective on the baptized person's participation in the death/resurrection of Christ to the experience of participation in the Eucharist. This is especially the case in those passages where Paul brings the two sacraments together, even if somewhat indirectly (e.g., 1 Cor 10:1ff): "The cup of blessing which we bless, is it not a participation in the blood of Christ? The bread which we break, is it not a participation in the body of Christ? Because there is one loaf, we who are many are one body, for we all partake of the same loaf."

In this passage the thought begins from the concrete situation of the worshipping community that is to partake in the breaking of the bread and in the cup. Paul chooses words that show a marked resemblance to the way in which he describes the fundamental meaning of Baptism in the same epistle. In chapter twelve of 1 Corinthians he speaks of how in Baptism all were baptized into one body through the one Spirit. (12:12-13). Therefore it seems indisputable that both of these central sacraments in the Christian tradition establish a sense of union with the body of believers who collectively, as well as individually, have experienced the Christ Event in its depths.

Thus far in this presentation our attention has been focused on the church's sacramental tradition for this is without doubt the principal locus of "remembering" in Christianity. But some mention also needs to be made of the festivals and festival seasons which assume great importance in the historic life of the churches. Advent and the Easter Vigil bear special scrutiny.

During the Advent season the church recalls the prophetic texts of the Hebrew Scriptures, understanding that they culminate in the birth of Jesus and what Christians have traditionally regarded as the final phase of the process of human redemption. But this is not mere historical recollection, as is evident when one examines many of the reflections of the church fathers on the significance of Advent. Here the message is clearly that there exists a threefold dimension of the church's liturgical celebration of Advent. The first is indeed the actual remembrance of the original historical birth. The third is the eschatological, the final coming of Christ. But the second dimension is the consciousness of the Christ entering the life of the believing community in the moment of actual celebration. Thus Advent/Christmas have always meant for the Christian believer a remembrance in which the present was every much as central as the past or future.

As similar approach predominates in the other two great liturgical festivals of the church year, Holy Week/Easter and Pentecost. Both look back and look ahead; but equally, they emphasize the experience of the Resurrection and the coming of the Spirit in the immediate life of the worshipping community.

This examination of the Christian approach to remembrance leaves us with several important questions, especially in an interreligious context. The very first one is whether, at least in the Western world, the kind of personal linkage with the central redemptive events in human history through remembrance that is pivotal for at least Christianity and Judaism may be in the process of serious, if not total, erosion under the impact of the Enlightenment's commitment to linear progress and the rapid growth of technology. If so, are Judaism and Christianity (and perhaps Islam as well) working out of a framework that is on the verge of collapse?

There is much evidence to suggest that the framework of our traditional religious approach to remembrance may be dying. But in my judgment it is still too soon to regard the situation as terminal. In a recent presentation to a meeting of the ethics faculty of the schools of the Association of Chicago Theological Schools Professor Steven Schroeder of St. Xavier College in Chicago turned our attention to the rediscovery of the power of "remembering" in contemporary literature. In a comparison of the thought of St. Augustine and the writings of Virginia Woolf Schroeder shows how these authors focused on memory in a way that was both complex and social. Of the two, he feels that Woolf may in fact be closer to the consciousness prevailing in the classical Christian liturgy than Augustine. What Woolf seems to evoke, according to Schroeder, is the sense that "memory" involves a cultural much more than a biological process. It is "a *cultural* act of remembering in which we become the media through which our cultures remember." The cultures to which we belong, he goes on to add, "'remember' us and 'remember' themselves *through* us."[11]

What writers such as Virginia Woolf may be telling us is that, despite appearance to the contrary, Western society has not lost all sense of the classical approach to memory found in Jewish and Christian liturgy. Even though the language and symbols of classical worship may be cast aside by modern writers, they may be preserving something of the basic framework. If so, hope of restoring a sense of liturgical remembrance may not be as futile a task as some would make it. The basic spark remains, however obscure its light.

The second and final challenge that confronts us regarding liturgical memory as Jews, Christians and Muslims who recognize a measure of linkage needs to be expressed in an explicit way in liturgical celebration. Obviously this issue presumes some positive response to the first challenge regarding the retrievability of the classical remembrance tradition. But on the assumption that such recovery is a possibility, are we not required to move on to ask if the central historically-based stories that form the centerpieces of our liturgical celebration should be incorporated in some way in each of our individual sacred rituals. If remembrance is the key to preservation of a living tradition much more than formal theology, then the liturgical setting becomes a decisive point of decision making regarding our basic attitudes towards one another.

In the Christian-Jewish dialogue there has been considerable talk of late, both in the writings of individual theologians as well as in certain church documents, about the inherent bonding that exists between the Church and the Jewish People. While neither Jews nor Christians have been quite prepared to make such a clear assertion with respect to Islam, there is nonetheless some growing understanding of an important bonding. What are the implication of these new interreligious theologies for the basic liturgical acts of remembrance around which our traditions turn. Surely we cannot say none if we hope to sustain the theological dialogue as something of importance.

Coming to grips with the religious tradition of remembrance clearly brings us back to the roots of our faith. But it also places before us some immeasurably difficult new problems that still await an adequate response. Hopefully our discussions throughout this day will move us at least a small way in terms of a solution.

Notes

1. Frank C. Senn, "Anamnesis," in Peter E. Fink, S.J. (ed.), *The New Dictionary of Sacramental Worship*. Collegeville, MN: The Liturgical Press (A Michael Glazier Book), 1990, 45-46.
2. Don E. Saliers, *Worship and Spirituality*. Philadelphia: Westminster, 1984, 19.
3. Saliers, *Worship*, 23.
4. Bastiaan van Iersel, S.M.M., "Some Biblical Roots of the Christian Sacrament," in Edward Schillebeeckx, O.P. and Boniface Willems, O.P., eds., *The Sacrament in General. Concilium*, vol. 31. New York/Glen Rock: Paulist Press, 1967, 9-10.
5. van Iersel, "Some Biblical Roots," 12.
6. cf. Frank Senn, "Anamnesis," *The New Dictionary of Sacramental Worship*, 45-46.
7. van Iersel, "Some Biblical Roots," 14.
8. Saliers, *Worship*, 62-63.
9. Saliers, *Worship*, 63.
10. cf. Paul van Buren, *Discerning the Way*. New York: Seabury, 1980; A *Christian Theology of the Jewish People*. New York: Seabury, 1983; and A *Theology of the Jewish Christian Reality, Part III: Christ in Context*. San Francisco: Harper & Row, 1988.
11. "Making Time: Some Ethical Reflections on the Subject in Virginia Woolf's 'A Sketch of the Past'," unpublished essay, presented to the Ethics Faculty Group Meeting, Association of Chicago Theological Schools, Catholic Theological Union, 13 February 1992, 11.

VIII

Faith as Memory: Theologies of the Jewish Holidays

BY BYRON L. SHERWIN

Losing one's memory means losing one's mind. To remember is to re-mind. Bereft of certain remembrances, one becomes *dis*membered from the divine, from one's own self, from one's past, from one's faith-community.[1]

For Judaism, faith is memory; recall of the past is a call to faith in the present. As Abraham Heschel has written:

> When we want to understand ourselves, to find out what is most precious in our lives, we search our memory. . . . That only is valuable in our experience which is worth remembering. Remembrance is the touchstone of all actions. Memory is a source of faith. To have faith is to remember. Jewish faith is a recollection of that which happened to Israel in the past . . . . Recollection is a holy act: we sanctify the present by remembering the past.[2]

No command to believe is stated in Hebrew Scripture. Rather, memory of events, of experience, is prescribed. The transmission of the faith-tradition from generation to generation is vested in the conveyance through memory of experienced events. For example, a verse in Deuteronomy (4:9) reads:

> Take heed to yourself diligently, lest you forget the things your eyes saw, and lest they depart from your heart all the days of your life, make them known to your children and your children's children.

The prophets of Israel did not formulate creedal propositions. Rather, they offered memories of moments illuminated by the divine presence. They did not enjoin the people of define God, but to witness the divine presence in history. God asked Israel to be a people of witnesses to God (Isa. 43:10), not a committee of definers of God.

In his classic work *Kuzari*, the medieval poet and philosopher Judah Halevi observed that the Ten Commandments do not begin with a creedal proposition, but with a memory of an experienced event: "I am the Lord your God who brought you out of the land of Egypt, out of the house of bondage" (Exod. 20:1). For Halevi, faith is rooted in the memory of events. Tradition's task is to transmit experience as memory.[3] Memory makes the past present, the future possible. The foundation for faith in the present is forged by the perpetuation of certain memories of the past. As Deuteronomy (32:7) tells us:

> Remember the days of old,
> Consider the years of ages past;
> Ask your father, he will inform you,
> Your elders, they will tell you.

Observance of many Jewish feasts and fasts offers a prime example of the nexus between faith and memory. Already in the biblical period, the process of transforming the nature-festivals of Mesopotamia into commemorations of remembered events in Israel's history had begun.[4] For example, the festival of "*Aviv*" (Spring) was transformed into Passover, a festival commemorating the Exodus from Egypt (see, e.g., Exod. 13, Deut. 16:3).

By the first century, it seems that the nature-festivals of Mesopotamia's polytheistic and pagan cult had been reformed to comply with the monotheistic and demythologized features of Israelite faith. Nature-festivals were celebrated as harvest festivals, with recognition of divine grace through sacrifice and celebration at the Temple in Jerusalem as a major motif. Commemoration of historical events was present, but not yet dominant. However, after the destruction of the (Second) Temple, the motif of memory and commemoration prevailed. Once severed from their land and from the temple cult, the Jews focused upon the historical features of the festivals. Indeed, in the diaspora even the Land and the Temple cult entered the orbit of the people's cherished memories.[5]

Rabbinic Judaism transformed Israelite faith into a historical religion. The memories of Israel's past were firmly embossed upon the festivals that comprised the Jewish liturgical year.[6] As the pre-eminent Jewish historian of our century, the late Salo W. Baron put it:

> It is well known, for instance, that the ancient Israelite festivals were taken over from the earlier cultures of Canaan and Babylonia. But in each case ancient Judaism changed the fundamental meaning of the festival first by adding to it, then by substituting for its natural an historical interpretation.[7]

Similarly, as Heschel observed:

> To Israel the unique events of historic time were spiritually more significant than the repetitive processes in the cycle of nature, even though physical sustenance depended upon the latter. While the deities of other peoples were associated with places or things, the God of Israel was the God of events: the Redeemer from slavery, the Revealer of the Torah, manifesting himself in the events of history rather than in things or places.[8]

Remembrances of the formative events in Israel's biblical past - the Exodus from Egypt and the revelation at Sinai, became prominent features of holyday observance. For example, the summer harvest festival, *Shavuot* or Pentecost, designated by Scripture as the "feast of ingathering" the wheat harvest and the summer fruits (Exod. 34:22, Numb. 28:26) became identified by the rabbis as the anniversary of the revelation of the Torah at Sinai.[9] The Jewish liturgy identifies this festival as "the time of the giving of the Torah."

The association of the Feast of Booths (Lev. 23:34) with the fall harvest was overshadowed by its identification with the booths in which the Israelites dwelt during their sojourn in the wilderness after the liberation from Egypt (Lev. 23:41-43). Though both the agricultural and the historical origins of this festival are stated by Scripture, the historical meaning subsequently became dominant. The "booth" was now more closely identified with historical memory of the desert experience, and less stongly identified with the booths in which the field-workers would dwell during the harvest. Here, too, nature gave way to history.

On Passover, the memory of the Exodus became the central motif. The Sabbath, the day of rest, is also associated with the Exodus. Slaves have no Sabbath. According to a verse in Deuteronomy (5:15), one should observe the Sabbath as a means of remembering Egyptian slavery and the liberation from bondage. While the Sabbath is also a commemoration of creation, the link with the memory of freedom from slavery provided an experiential referent that reference to creation could not offer, i.e., Israel participated in the Exodus, but only God witnessed the creation of the world. The Jewish liturgy for the Sabbath preserves referents both to the Exodus and to Creation.[10]

Holydays such as *Purim*, the Feast of Lots, *Hanukah* and *Tisha B'Av* had clear historical references from the outset of their celebration. Purim refers to the events narrated in the biblical story of Esther. Hanukah refers to the liberation from oppression by Syrian Hellenists. *Tisha B'Av* is linked to the destruction of Temple in Jerusalem as well as to other tragedies in Jewish history.[11] Even the apparently a-historical occasion of the Jewish New Year (*Rosh ha-Shanah*), denoted by Scripture as a Day of Remembrance (Lev. 23:24) (though the object of remembrance is not stated) is described by the talmudic rabbis and later by the liturgy either as the anniversary of the creation of the world or as the anniversary of the creation of the first human being.[12]

Reflection upon the role of remembrance in the Jewish liturgical years yields a variety of insights into the nature of Jewish faith. Because faith is articulated as memory, and because memory of the formative events of ancient Jewish history are identified with the Jewish holydays, it should not be surprising to find that central concepts of Jewish theological concern are associated with the religious festivals. Thus, the structure of Jewish theology is not systematic, but liturgical. As the nineteenth-century rabbi Samson Raphael Hirsch put it, the Jewish liturgy is Judaism's catechism. Celebration of the Jewish festivals conveys the Jewish theological agenda. For example, Passover relates to redemption, Pentecost to revelation, *Sukkot* (the Feast of Booths) to divine providence, Sabbath to creation, *Tisha B'Av* to theodicy.[13]

Theological concepts and concerns are not permitted to remain abstract propositions. Rather, they are communicated as specific memories through festivals of celebration and remembrance. For Judaism, theological concepts never atrophy into abstract creeds because they are continuously being vocalized through deeds. The function of rituals associated with the various Jewish holydays is to internalize in the life of each member of the people the memory of an event in the life of the people. Consider, for examle, this citation from the Passover *Haggadah*:

> In each generation, each individual should consider himself or herself as if he or she was redeemed from Egypt, as it is said, "It is because of what God did for *me* when *I* went free from Egypt" (Exod. 13:8). For the Holy One redeemed not only our ancestors, but *us with them*, as it is said, "God took *us* out of there to bring us to the land promised to our ancestors" (Deut. 6:23). Therefore, we must . . . praise God who . . . took *us* from slavery to freedom.[14]

The liturgy for the *Seder*, the Passover meal, is called *Haggadah*, "telling." This relates to the biblical injunction to pass down memories of experience to one's children: "You shall tell your child on that day: It is because of what the Lord did for me when I went free from Egypt" (Exod. 13:8). History is remebered; it is retold; but it is not re-enacted. Tradition is passed down by the telling within linear time. Re-enactment, on the other hand, aims at obliterating time. The goal in Jewish ritual is to remember and not to re-enact an event.[15] The uniqueness of the event can be recited, but not repeated. However, what can be re-enacted is the *meaning* of the event. Indeed, for the tradition to continue, for the story to have perpetual and perpetuated meaning, it must be internalized.[16]

By the internalization of memory through ritual, we become our ancestors' contemporaries. Present and past converge at the moment of celebration and commemoration. Memory is the stimulus, and, ritual and liturgy are the vehicle that bind past and present, ancestor and descendant, ancient experience and contemporary faith.

The expectation that commemoration of the Exodus would bring about a personal as well as a communal experience of liberation is expressed by the hasidic master, Nahum of Tchernoble. He suggests that two types of liberation are necessary for Passover observance to be considered complete. One type celebrates the liberation of Israel from Egypt. The second type is the liberation of each person from that particular thing that enslaves him or her. Unless the individual liberates himself or herself from his or her own particular Egypt, the celebration of Passover is not complete.[17]

The Hebrew word for memory is "*zakhar*." But, memory does not merely signify mental recall, but includes a call to action. Not affirmation of dogmas but evocation of deeds is the meaning of this term. Liturgy and ritual serve as vehicles to prevent memory from deteriorating into an abstract reminiscence. Remembrance through observance of the festivals stifles the proclivity toward abstract theological speculation, toward intellectual voyeurism devoid of commitment. As Abraham Heschel put it, "An esthetic experience leaves behind the memory of a perception and enjoyment; a prophetic experience leaves behind the memory of commitment."[18]

In his analysis of the syntax of the word "*zakhar*" - "remembrance" in Hebrew Scripture, the biblical scholar J. Pedersen observed that "*zakhar*" does not refer to an "objective memory image of some thing or event, but that this image is called forth in the soul and assists in determining its action. . . . Therefore, *zakhar* may also mean to begin an action, to proceed to something, as when Elihu says, 'Proceed (*zekhor*) to magnify God's work, which people sing of' (Job 36:24)."[19]

This understanding of "*zakhar*" as memory pregnant with action, as memory as a directional signal for the performance of particular deeds, is found in a variety of classical Jewish sources. For example, in the first hasidic book, the *Toledot Ya'akov Yoseif*, Jacob Joseph of Polnoye wrote: "In every place in Scripture where one finds the commandment to remember, one is commanded to perform a specific deed whereby one links memory to action, as in the commandment of the fringes (see Numb. 15:37-41) and those like it which are like a knot (on one's finger to remind one) not to forget (to do something)."[20]

Memory is a call to action, to commemoration. However, the call is directed to those who share a memory of an event. For example, the command to commemorate the Exodus is addressed to those who experienced. it. As the text in Exodus reads:

> This day shall be for you one of remembrance; you shall celebrate it as an institution for all time (Exod. 12:14) . . . .
>
> Remember this day, on which you went free from Egypt, the house of bondage, how the Lord freed you from it with a mighty hand; no leavened bread shall be eaten (Exod. 13:3) . . . . And you shall explain it to your son on that day: It is because of what the Lord did for me when I went free from Egypt (Exod. 13:8) (also see Deut. 16:1-8).

In this view, participation in the life of the faith-community is a prerequisite for commemorating events in the history of that faith-community. For example the Passover liturgy tells of four sons. Of these, the wicked son asks:

> "What does this ritual mean to you? (Exod.12:26), i.e., to you and not to him. Since he excludes himself from the community and denies God's role in the

> Exodus, you should confront him and say: "This is done because of what God did for me when I went out to Egypt" (Exod. 13:8). For me and not for him. Had he been there he would not have been redeemed.

Rejection of the memories bequeathed to us is a form of spiritual self-disinheritance. One can only pity the person who fails to hear the melody of the memory. In this regard, commenting on the biblical description of revelation of the Torah at Sinai, the hasidic master Moses Hayyim Ephraim of Sedlykow, told this tale:

> A certain man played so exquisitely on a violin that anyone who heard his playing could not be restrained from dancing. The closer one was to the sound of the music, the stronger the urge to dance and the greater one's pleasure and joy from the music. Once a deaf person came around. He did not see the person playing the violin, and because he was deaf, he could not hear the music. All he saw were people dancing in joy and ecstacy. He muttered to himself, "They are mad. They are mad."[21]

Participation in the life of a faith-community means participation in its memories. It entails being able to discern the nuances of its medley of memories. To participate means to act, to observe, to celebrate. Memories are pregnant with action. Memories that do not stimulate action are stillborn. For Judaism, there is no faith without correlative deeds, without observance of ritual and law (*halakhah*).

The continuity of a faith-community depends upon its ability to perpetuate its memories. Memory is then simply the retelling of what we once knew, of what we once experienced. According to a midrash, the souls of all future generations of Jews stood at Siani with the generation of the Exodus to receive the Torah. The hasidic master Elimelekh of Lizensk once said, "I not only remember the giving of the Torah at Sinai, I even remember who stood next to me then and there."[22] More recently, an Israeli newspaper told the story of two strangers who meet on a crowded bus in Tel Aviv. One says to the other, "Don't I know you from somewhere?" The other facetiously says, "Maybe we stood together at Sinai." The more friendly stranger holds out his hand and says. "You must be right. How have you been all of this time?"

Tradition is selective in terms of which memories of which events it seeks to emphasize and to perpetuate. Consequently *heilsgeschichte* ("sacred history") and not *historische wissenschaft* ("scientific history") determines the contours of memories of past events, and selects which memories are to play a role in the liturgical life of the faith-community. The works that constitute the sacred canon, rather than archaeological discoveries or the claims of extra-canonical works or the products of philological-historical method decide how the past is to be understood by and transmited to the future. Thus, while memory engenders faith, faith shapes memory. Faith forms memory by selecting the significant, by determining what is to be remembered, and how it is to be remembered. Faith forms and transforms memory. Memory both stimulates and transmits faith.

The demilitarization of Jewish memory by rabbinic tradition may serve as an example of how faith shapes memory. For instance, there are no Jewish festivals commemorating military victories. Joshua's defeat of the Canaanites, David's conquest of Jerusalem, and Samson's victory over the Philistines, have no liturgical referents.

What about Hanukah? Is Hanukah not rooted in the memory of the military victories of the Maccabees? Do not the Books of the Maccabees and Josephus recount these military victories and relate them to Hanukah? They do. However, this is not the story tradition sought to remember.

The story of the military victory of the Maccabees is not preseved in Jewish canonical literature. The books of the Maccabees are outside the canon. They are apocryphal, i.e., non-canonical. The talmudic discussions of Hanukah focus on the miracle of the single cruze of oil in the desecrated Temple that lasted eight days rather than one day.[23] Hanukah became a festival of lights, not of fights. The liturgy recalls those who remained faithful to the Torah in times of oppression rather than the military exploits of the Maccabees. Indeed, God-and not the Maccabees - is described as the one who vanquishes the enemy.[24] The liturgy focuses on the miracle not on the military, on divine providence and not on successful military strategies. Indeed, classical Jewish religious literature stresses the ideological rather than the military conflict in its discussion of Hanukah.[25] The emphasis is upon the battle of ideologies - Judaism vs. Hellensim, totalitarianism vs. liberty, and not upon the battle of armies.

While memory is a dominant theme in the celebration of the Jewish festivals, expectation also plays a role. In linking memory to expectation, past and future converge in the present. For example, the ram's horn (*shofar*) blown on the Jewish New Year is as much a reminder of the blasts characteristic of the expected messianic redemption as they are the recalled revelation at Sinai. The redemption from Egypt is the precedent upon which faith in the final messianic redemption is predicated. Here one encounters a polarity between memory and expectation, between remembrance of historical events and hopes for a time that brings history to its eschatological conclusion.[26] For example, the Sabbath is a commemoration both of the beginning and of the end. It is both a remembrance of creation and a "foretaste of the World to Come."[27] Or, as Martin Buber said, "He who does not himself remember that God led him out of Egypt, he who does not himself await the Messiah, is no longer a true Jew."[28]

While memory of past events serves as a call to action, so does the evocation of other types of remembrance. For example, the biblical injunction of remembrance regarding the New Year has no specific historical referent. A verse in Leviticus (23:24) reads: "In the seventh month, on the first day of the month, you shall observe a complete rest, a sacred occasion commemorated with loud blasts." While, as was noted, some rabbinic and liturgical texts relate the New Year to the creation of the world or to the creation of the first human being, and while others relate the "loud blasts" to the revelation at Sinai, still other sources posit an a-historical referent for memory. For instance, some texts relate remembrance to the demand that the individual remember his or her sins, his or her covenantal commitment, and seek reconciliation with the divine through repentance. The blast of the ram's horn may be compared to an alarm clock, awakening the awareness of the need for self-scrutiny and self-improvement. Other texts, particularly liturgical ones, interpret the biblical call to remembrance as a call to God to recall the steadfast faith of one's ancestors and to apply their merit to the penitent's deficit of good deeds. One asks God to remember him or her with grace and forgiveness when determining one's fate on the basis of an evaluation of one's deeds.[29]

The Hebrew word "*zakhar*" means not only "memory" but "male." This observation was utilized by the medieval Jewish mystics to provide the celebration of the Jewish holydays with an additional level of meaning. For the kabbalists, the main purpose of human action is not anthropocentric but theocentric. They developed ideas found in earlier rabbinic texts that considered human actions as opportunites for rectifying and repairing the shattered cosmos, and more particularly the Godhead itself. For the Jewish mystics, each act has the ability either to help further to fragment the divine, either to accelerate or to retard the messianic advent. For the kabbalists, human action has theosophical-theurgic implications and effects.[30]

According to the Jewish mystics, there are "masculine" and "feminine" elements within the Godhead (i.e., the *Sefirot*). Human actions may affect the desired reunification and harmony of these elements; or, they may bring about an undesirable disaffection and conflict between these elements. Observance of the laws and commandments stimulates harmony, while sin increases disharmony.

The medieval Jewish mystics both amplified the meaning of already existing rituals related to holyday observance and introduced new rituals for holyday observance. Many of these relate to the goal of inducing harmony between the "male" and "female" features of the divine personality. A paradigmatic example relates to Sabbath observance.[31]

In the version of the Ten Commandments found in Exodus (20:8), one is enjoined to "remember" the Sabbath day. Here we have the word "*zakhor*" which the kabbalists understood as a double entendre, referring both to remembrance and to maleness. In the Deuteronimic version of the Ten Commandments, the command is to "observe" or to "guard" (*shamor*) the Sabbath day (Deut. 5:12). The medieval kabbalistic text, *Sefer ha-Bahir* observes:

> Why is it said: "Remember the Sabbath" and "Observe the Sabbath?" "Remember" ("*zakhor*") refers to the male ("*zakhar*") and "observe" refers to the female.[32]

According to the kabbalists, the goal of Sabbath observance is to bring about the reunification of the male and female aspects of the divine.[33] In kabbalistic literature, one encounters similar views regarding the meaning of observance of the other Jewish holydays.[34] The *zivvuga kaddisha*-"sacred coupling" (in the parlance of the Zohar) has certain similarities with hierogamy or *hieros gamos* known in other religious traditions.[35] However, one can detect a different focus in kabbalistic texts. While many other traditions portray the "sacred marriage" as an imitation of the divine coupling, the kabbalists perceive humanly performed sacred deeds as stimulating the divine coupling. For the kabbalists, human activity - particularly sexual activity - is theurgic and not imitative. The goal of the kabbalist is not to mimic but to transform the divine. By effecting a re-union of the male and female elements of the divine through the performance of sacred deeds related to holyday observance, the individual celebrant stimulates the influx of divine blessing into the world.

By adding this layer of meaning upon the observance of the Jewish holydays, the kabbalists provided a rubric of meaning that might be applied even to those holydays unrelated either by history or interpretation to memories of past events. One example is the celebration of the New Moon, a festival related not to history but to nature, to a cyclical event rather than to linear time. The moon is related by the kabbalists to the *Shekhinah* - the feminine aspect of the divine. The goal is to liberate Moon/*Shekhinah* from exile, and to restore her to her original fullness. The liberation of the moon from her cosmic exile would then be reflected in the end of Israel's terresrial exile which is identified with the advent of messianic redemption.[36] Thus, while the medieval kabbalists shifted the focus of holyday observance from the anthropocentric to the theocentric, from memory to theurgy, they did not abandon the focus on history. Indeed, a central goal of the kabbalists was to encourage through observance the acceleration of history towards its eventual messianic climax.

Before concluding this discussion of the Jewish holydays, reference should be made to a number of contemporary trends of understanding and observing the Jewish holydays.

Each generation of Jews has perceived a contemporary meaning in the paradigms of the past embodied in the holydays. Indeed, the continuity of tradition has largely been assured by the ability of each generation to perceive its contemporary situation in the mirror of tradition. As Rabbi Abraham Isaac Kuk put it, "The Torah is like a mirror. Like a mirror, the Torah always stays the same, but each generation sees its own reflection, a different reflection, in the same mirror."

Throughout the generations, in many different lands, the Passover paradigm of captivity and freedom, or the Hanukah paradigm of religious oppresssion and subsequent liberation, was perceived in terms of past as prologue, memory of the past as contemporary experience. With specific reference to today, it is not coincidential that the massive efforts currently being expended by American Jewry on the emigration of Jews from the former Soviet Union is called "Operation Exodus."

Each generation identified a contemporary figure with Haman - a demagogue desiring the annihilation of the Jewish people. Torquemada, Chemelnitzki and Hitler, were perceived as contemporary reincarnations of Haman, the perennial and archenemy of the Jews. The festival of Purim serves as an annual reminder that a Haman lurks waiting to attack in each generation. The constant hope is that as Haman was defeated so will be his later incarnations. In January 1991, the new Haman was perceived to be Sadam Hussein. That the Gulf War ended at the time of Purim was seen by many Jews as a contemporary version of the biblical tale. According to midrash, "Rabbi Nathan said: Haman came to serve as a reminder for all generations, as it is said, 'These days of Purim should not fail from among the Jews, nor the memory of them perish from their descendants' (Esther 9:28)."[37]

The two formative events for contemporary Jewry are the Holocaust and the establishment of the State of Israel. Response to these events by world Jewry has led to a number of significant changes in the celebration of the Jewish liturgical year. One example is the initiation of new Jewish holydays, such as *Yom ha-Atzma'ut* (Israel Independence Day), *Yom ha-Shoah* (Holocaust Memorial Day), and primarily in Israel *Yom Yerushalayim* (Jerusalem Day) celebrating the reunification of Jerusalem during the 1967 war.[38]

That new Jewish holydays have been established for the first time in hundreds of years demonstrates the profound significance afforded the events they commemorate. That these holydays have received the endorsement and encouragement of much of the Orthodox rabbinate, a group largely ideologically resistant to change and innovation, is significant. Nonetheless, a number of problematic issues with regard to these new holydays merit mention.

One such issue is the introduction into the Jewish liturgical year of celebrations of military victories as such. While David's conquest of Jerusalem did not lead to the establishment of a commemorative festival, the 1967 reunification of Jerusalem did. This is but one indication of how the demilitarization of the Jewish liturgical year imposed by rabbinic and medieval tradition is currently being uprooted and reversed.

This new approach to telling and remembering Jewish history and to celebrating certain events that comprise it has led to a retelling of past events, a revisioning of memory, a restructuring of the meaning of the Jewish liturgical year. As Liebman and Don-Yehiya have observed correctly in their insightful study *Civil Religion in Israel*, there must be an inevitable clash between traditional Jewish symbols and values and those of Israel's "civil religion:" "The symbols and values, expressed in traditional forms, conflict with the needs and values of the modern state."[39]

One example of the transformation of the traditional focus of festival observance and meaning relates to Hanukah. Originally a "minor" holiday in the Jewish liturgical year, it has become in recent generations a major festival. In America, this seems to have occurred because Jews felt a need to have a counterpart to Christmas. In Israel, this seems to have occurred because Hanukah could be easily reinterpreted to conform with the dogmas of the civil religion of the State of Israel.

As was noted above, the talmudic rabbis and the medievals largely demilitarized Hanukah. The war of the Hasmoneans was downplayed while the miracle of the oil and the rededication of the sanctuary were stressed. Indeed, Hanukah means "rededication." The clashes on the battlefield were minimized; the clash of ideologies - Judaism vs. Hellenism, was emphasized. When the liturgy speaks about the Maccabean triumph, it assigns the victory to divine intervention rather than to military acumen. However, in the civil religion of Israel, the military victory becomes the central motif. A religious holiday is transformed into a primarily national holiday. The Maccabees and not God are awarded the victory. The rededication of the Sanctuary is all but forgotten. Not divine redemption but self-redemption through military skill is stressed. The Maccabees are presented not as fighters for religious freedom or for the preservation of Jewish religious life and thought, but as patriots, as guerillas rebelling against military occuation and national subjugation.[40] The past is viewed as a prologue: the I.D.F. (Israel Defense Forces) are considered the Maccabees of our generation. The victory of the Maccabees over the Syrians becomes the precedent for the defeat of Syria in modern Israel' wars. The past is understood in terms compatible with the *realpolitik* of today's Middle East conflict.

Even *Yom ha-Shoah* has been given a military focus. In Israel, the official name of this commemoration is *Yom ha-Shoah ve-ha-Gevurah* - the "Day of Holocaust and Heroism," with increasing importance being afforded Jewish armed resistance during the Second World War - with the Warsaw Ghetto uprising often perceived in Israel as the prelude to the formation of the Israel Defense Forces, as a paradigm rather than as an exception to Jewish responses to Nazism.[41] It is further significant that commemoration of the Holocaust was not subsumed under previously established Jewish holydays commemorating national disasters, such as the Ninth of Av (*Tisha B'Av*) - the day commemorating the destruction of the Temples and numerous other castastrophes. This may be grounded in the perception of the Holocaust as a unique, unparalleled and incomparable event in Jewish experience. Nevertheless, the choice of 27 Nissan as the date for *Yom ha-Shoah* is curious since there is no signficant referent for that date in the annals of the history of the Holocaust. While some associate that date with the Warsaw Ghetto uprising, the date of *Yom ha-Shoah* does not exactly coincide with any significant date related to the uprising. What is also noteworthy is that the Ninth of Av does in fact coincide with a significant date in Holocaust history, namely, the initiation of the use of the gas chambers at Treblinka (which, unlike Auschwitz, was almost exclusively involved with the mass murder of Jews to the exclusion of members of other national or religious groups).[42] In this regard, one may speculate that the realtionship on the calendar between *Yom ha-Shoah* and *Yom ha-Atzma'ut* (the latter occurs a week after the former) articulates a major dogma of the current "civil religion" of Israel, and of the "civil religion" of American Jewry, namely, linking the Holocaust to the emergence of Israel, death to rebirth, murder to resurrection.[43] In a sense, the relation of *Yom-ha-Shoah* to *Yom ha-Atzma'ut* might be interpreted as a Jewish parallel to Good Friday and Easter.

In the United States, growing concern for ecological issues, and, in Israel the civil religion have encouraged a shift of focus from history back to nature with regard to the observance of certain Jewish holydays. For example, Zionist ideology's emphasis upon the rebuilding of the land of Israel through agricultural development, predictably led to the return to the biblical or even the pre-biblical view of the holydays as being primarily nature-festivals. Particularly among the "secular" Israelis, this has brought about a desacralization, even a "repaganization" of the Jewish festivals.[44] Furthermore, as was already noted, the remilitarization and nationalization of the meaning of traditional Jewish holydays, inevitably has led to their de-theologization.

In my view, the growing secularization of Judaism, evident in contemporary interpretations of the Jewish festivals, poses a profound threat to the continuity of Jewish faith. Theological concepts endemic to Jewish faith are being ignored or forgotten. Traditional memories are being cast into oblivion, or recast beyond recognition. Religious festivals are being purged of their religious meaning. Nationalistic themes are replacing theological motives. It is therefore not surprising that a recent demographic study found that in the United States 95% of those surveyed who identified as Jews did not see commitment to Judaism as *the* essential component of their Jewish identity.[45]

Jewish continuity is in danger, not because of antisemitism from without, but because of a progressive amnesia from within the Jewish community. As Abraham Heschel put it, "We are like messengers who have forgotten the message." The late Nobel laureate for literature, Isaac Bashevis Singer, used to say that Jews suffer from many diseases, but amnesia is not one of them. However, I am afraid he was wrong.[46]

Unless Jews recapture and preseve their memories, they will do to themselves what massacres, pogroms and Holocaust were unable to accomplish - to obliterate Judaism, to make of it a forgotten memory. Again, to quote Heschel:

> The tasks, begun by the partriarchs and prophets and continued by their descendants, are now entrusted to us. We are either the last Jews or those who will hand over the entire past to generations to come. We either forfeit or enrich the legacy of the ages. . . . We of this generation are still holding the key [to the sanctuary hidden in the realm of spirit.] Unless we remember, unless we unlock it, the holiness of the ages will remain a secret of God.[47]

Notes

1. According to hasidic theology, each Jew is "*aiver ha-Shekhinah*," a "limb of God," a "divine member." This is similar to the Christian idea that in being part of the Church, one is part of the *Corpus Christi*, the Body of Christ. Dismemberment means separation from the divine. For Judaism, remembrance is an entrée to rememberment.
2. Abraham Joshua Heschel, *Man is Not Alone* (Philadelphia: Jewish Publication Society, 1951), pp. 162-163.
3. Judah Halevi, *Kuzari*, Hartwig Hirschfield, trans. (New York: Schocken, 1964), 1:21-26, pp. 46-47.
4. See, e.g., Helmer Ringgren, *Israelite Religion* (Philadelphia: Fortress Press, 1966), p. 51.

5. I deliberately have chosen not to discuss the celebration of the festivals in biblical times, such as those connected with the Temple cult of those that may have predated the Temple cult. Nor have I chosen to discuss the various intriguing theories regarding biblical "enthronement" or "re-enactment" rituals, many of which have been put forth by the "Swedish School" of modern biblical scholarship. The reason for this choice is not because these issues lack significance, but because, in my view, they lack a certain relevance to a theological exposition of the Jewish holydays. Though it has often been said, it is nonetheless necessary to state again that Judaism is not equivalent to Hebrew Scripture. Rather, Judaism is how Jewish tradition interpreted Hebrew Scripture. Consequently, the focus of my attention is on the meaning of the Jewish holydays within the context of classical Jewish religious interpretation, primarily during the talmudic and medieval periods.
6. On the festivals in rabbinic literature, see, e.g., George Foot Moore, *Judaism* (Cambridge: Harvard University Press, 1927), vol. 2, pp. 40-69, see esp., p. 48.
7. Salo W. Baron, A *Social and Religious History of the Jews, vol. 1* (New York: Columbia University Press, 1952), p. 5. For a more popular view, see, e.g., Hayyim Schauss, *The Jewish Festivals* (New York: Union of American Hebrew Congregations, 1938), esp. pp. 43-44.
8. Abraham Joshua Heschel, *The Sabbath* (New York: World, 1963), p. 63. Compare this discussion to Eliade's paradigm of the "archaic man" who refuses "to accept himself as a historical being, his refusal to grant value to memory and hence to the unusual event." See Mircea Eliade, *Cosmos and History* (New York: Harper, 1959), p. 85. On the "God of the Jewish people . . . who carelessly intervenes in history, who reveals his will through events," see p. 104. See also Eliade, *The Sacred and the Profane* (New York: Harper, 1961), p. 110, "For Judaism, time has a beginning and will have an end. The idea of cyclical time is left behind." See also e.g., Monford Harris, "History, Memory, Action," *Conservative Judaism* 26:4 (Summer 1972): 58-63.
9. See, e.g., *Pesahim* 68b; *Exodus Rabbah* 31:16. In the *Guide of the Perplexed* (3:43), Maimonides succinctly states, "The Pentecost is the day of the giving of the Torah." See Louis Finkelstein, *The Pharisees* (Philadelphia: Jewish Publication Society, 1966), pp. 115-118.
10. See, e.g., the *kiddush* (blessing over wine) for the Sabbath.
11. See, e.g., *Taanit* 26b, 29a. Traditions also relate *Tisha B'Av* to events such as Moses' shattering of the Ten Commandments, the destruction of the fortress at Betar, and the expulsion of the Jews from Spain in 1492 (i.e., August 2, 1492 which corresponded that year with *Tisha B'Av*).
12. On *Rosh ha-Shanah* as Adam's "birthday," see e.g., *Leviticus Rabbah* 29:1; as the birthday of the biblical patriarchs, see e.g., *Rosh ha-Shanah* 10b. The liturgy for *Rosh ha-Shanah (musaf-amidah)* states "Today is the birthday of the world." This also seems to be based on *Rosh ha-Shanah* 10b.
13. Three Jewish thinkers who relate fundamental ideas of Jewish theology to the holydays are the fifteenth-century Spanish commentator Isaac Arama, the sixteenth-century kabbalist, Judah Loew of Prague, and the early twentieth-century German philosopher, Franz Rosenzweig. See Isaac Arama, *Akedat Yitzhak* (Pressburgh, 1849), Sermon No. 67, p. 99b. Arama relates six theological concepts to the festivals listed in Lev. 23, as follows: Sabbath-creation, Passover-God's power, *Shavuot*-revelation, *Rosh ha-Shanah* - providence, *Yom Kippur* -repentance, *Sukkot* - immortality. See the discussion of Arama by Menahem Kellner, *Dogma in Medieval Jewish Thought* (New York: Oxford University Press, 1986), pp. 159-161. On Judah Loew, see, e.g., Byron L. Sherwin, *Mystical Theology and Social Dissent* (New York: Oxford University Press, 1982), pp. 39-40. Rosenzweig relates the Sabbath and the "pilgrimage festivals" to creation, revelation and redemption. See Franz Rosenzweig,

The Star of Redemption, William H. Hallo, trans. (New York: Holt, Rinehart & Winston, 1970), pp. 308-328.

14. This text in the *Haggadah* is based on M. *Pesahim* 10:5, 6. See the insightful analysis by Baruch M. Bokser, *The Origins of the Seder* (Berkeley: University of California Press, 1984), pp. 86-87.
15. See, e.g., the illuminating study by Monford Harris, "The Passover Seder: On Entering the Order of History," *Judaism* 25:2 (Spring 1976): 167-174.
16. Certain Jews, such as Yemenites and Russian Caucasians, do "re-enact" the Exodus as part of their Passover observance. However, this is an ethnic curiosity rather than a normative practice.
17. Menahem Nahum of Tchernoble, *Ma'or Einayim* (Jerusalem, 1966), "*Tzav*," pp. 130-131.
18. Abraham Joshua Heschel, *God in Search of Man* (New York: Harper, 1955), p. 212.
19. Johannes Pedersen, *Israel: Its Life and Culture* (London: Oxford University Press, 1926), vol. 1, pp. 106-107.
20. Jacob Joseph of Polnoye, *Toledot Ya'akov Yoseif* (Jerusalem, 1967), "*Mattot*," p. 598. See also, Zohar III, 93b.
21. Moses Hayyim Epharim of Sedlykow, *Degel Mahaneh Ephraim* (Jerusalem: Hadar, 1963), "*Yitro*," p. 111.
22. *Sefer Ohel Elimelekh* (Jerusalem, 1968), para. 63, p. 8b.
23. See *Shabbat* 21b.
24. This is also true of Passover. Some have explained the absence of mention of Moses in the Passover *Haggadah* as being related to the tradition's stress upon God's exclusive role in redemption, to the exclusion of human efforts or human agents. For example, the Passover *Haggadah* states, "God took us out of Egypt not by an angel, not be a seraf, not by a messenger; rather the Holy One Himself." A similar sentiment regarding the redemption of the people celebrated on Purim and Hanukah is found in the "*al-ha-Nisim*" prayers recited on those festivals.
25. See, e.g., the discussion of the meaning of Hanukah offered by Judah Loew of Prague in his *Ner Mitzvah* (B'nai Brak, Israel: Yahadut, 1962).
26. See, e.g., the discussion in *Rosh ha-Shanah* 11a of when the final redemption will come and how it will occur in the same month as the liberation from Egypt. In the Sefardic *musaf-Kedushah*, reference is made to God saying, "I will redeem you in the end as in the beginning." According to Saadya Gaon, a rational reason for expecting God's final redemption is because of the precedent set by the redemption from Egypt; see his *Emunot ve-Deot (Beliefs and Opinions)*, 8:1.
27. See, e.g., *Berakhot* 57b.
28. Quoted in Will Herberg, ed., *The Writings of Martin Buber* (New York: World, 1961), p. 31.
29. On these themes, see the liturgy for *Rosh ha-Shanah* and *Yom Kippur*, e.g., in the "reader's repetition" of the *Amidah* prayer for *musaf*.
30. On the theosophical and theurgic motives as being dominant in Jewish mystical thought, see Moshe Idel, *Kabbalah: New Perspectives* (New Haven: Yale University Press, 1988).
31. On the Sabbath in Jewish mysticism, see the thorough study by Elliot Ginsburg, *The Sabbath in Classical Kabbalah* (Albany: SUNY Press, 1989).
32. *Sefer ha-Bahir*, Reuven Margaliot, ed. (Jerusalem: Mosad ha-Rav Kook, 1951), para. 181, p. 79. See also Zohar I, 48b.
33. See, e.g., the discussion in Tishbi's classic work, *Mishnat ha-Zohar* now available in English translation: Isaiah Tishbi, *The Wisdom of the Zohar*, David Goldstein, trans. (London: Oxford University Press, 1989), pp. 1223-1228. Also see Ginsburg, pp. 69-74, 101-122.
34. See Tishbi, pp. 1238-1259 and sources noted there. Note, Gershom Scholem, *On the Kabbalah and Its Symbolism* (New York: Schocken, 1965), pp. 137-146.

35. See, e.g., Mircea Eliade, *The Myth of the Eternal Return* (Princeton: Princeton University Press, 1965), pp. 23-27.
36. See, e.g.,Scholem, *On the Kabbalah and Its Symbolism*, pp. 151-152.
37. *Mekhilta de Rabbi Yishmael*, Jacob Lauterbach, ed. (Philadelphia: Jewish Publication Society, 1933), "*Amalek*," 2, vol. 2, p. 159.
38. On *Yom ha-Atzma'ut*, see, e.g., Shelomo Goren, *Torat ha-Moadim* (Tel Aviv: Zioni, 1964), pp. 568-598. On *Yom ha-Atzma'ut* and *Yom Yerushalayim*, see, e.g., Charles S. Liebman and Eliezer Don-Yehiya, *Civil Religion in Israel* (Berkeley: University of California Press, 1983), pp. 153-155.
39. Liebman and Don-Yehiya, p. 16. Also see their extensive discussion and analysis of the reinterpretation of the Jewish liturgical year according to the civil religion of Israel.
40. Liebman and Don-Yehiya, pp. 52-53.
41. See e.g., Amos Elon, *The Israelis* (New York: Holt, Rinehart & Winston, 1971), p. 206; Liebman and Don-Yehiya, pp. 151-153.
42. On the problematics of the date for *Yom ha-Shoah*, see, e.g., Abraham P. Bloch, *The Biblical and Historical Background of the Jewish Holy Days* (New York: Ktav, 1978), pp. 253-258. Bloch recommends *Lag Ba'Omer*, the traditional festival of rejoicing because of a respite from catastrophe, as a proper day for *Yom ha-Shoah* as that coincides with the anniversary of Hitler's death. On Treblinka and *Tisha B'Av*, see Nora Levin, *The Holocaust* (New York: Schocken, 1973), p. 319. In 1942 *Tisha B'Av* corresponded to July 23.
43. For an extensive presentation of the civil religion of American Jews, see Jonathan S. Woocher, *Sacred Survival: The Civil Religion of American Jews* (Bloomington, Ind.: Indiana University Press, 1986), esp. pp. 131-157.
44. The "back to nature" theme in Zionist ideology is too complex for discussion here. The "return to the Bible" must be understood as a nationalistic trend, and not a religious one. Indeed, it articulates a rejection of talmudic and medieval rabbinic authority, often identified by Zionist ideologists with the "abnormal" diasporan Jewish experience.
45. *Highlights of the Council of Jewish Federations 1990 National Jewish Population Study* (New York: Council of Jewish Federations, 1991), p. 28. "Further analysis shows that less than 5 percent of all respondents consider being Jewish solely in terms of being a member of a religious group, whereas 90 percent define being Jewish as being a member of a cultural or ethnic group."
46. On the discontinuity of Jewish memory in the modern period, and the problems it poses, see the insightful work by Yosef Hayim Yerushalmi, *Zakhor: Jewish History and Jewish Memory* (Seattle: University of Washington Press, 1982). On p. 93, Yersuhalmi writes, "Only in the modern era do we really find, for the first time, a Jewish historiography divorced from Jewish collective memory and, in crucial respects, thoroughly at odds with it."
47. Abraham Joshua Heschel, *The Earth is the Lord's* (New York: Schumann, 1951), p. 107.

IX

Mixed Blessings: Martin Luther King, Jr., Memory and the Lessons of an Ambiguous Heroism

BY MICHAEL E. DYSON

The establishment of a national holiday to honor the life and achievements of Martin Luther King, Jr., is a reason for critical celebration. Only the second American and first African-American to be feted with this singular honor, the celebration of King's birthday is an occasion of national, religious and racial significance. It acknowledges that King was the supreme embodiment of American citizenship and political engagement, the highest manifestation of the American religious genius, and the richest expression of the multifaceted character of the black experience in America.

On the other hand, the King birthday celebration also presents the danger of losing the challenging and uncomfortable dimensions of King's thought and life by romanticizing his career. The nature and scope of King's accomplishments, which center in nothing short of a specific revolution in how black people live and are perceived in American culture, inevitably invite historic embellishment and social myth. But neither a puerile romanticization of King as Safe Negro, nor a caricatured mythologization of King as Great American Hero will do. King's life was too complex, his achievements too profound and his thinking too provocative to warrant such naive responses. We must transcend such unrealistic assessments of King and concentrate on the substantive contributions of his life and thought.

An especially helpful and illuminating way to view King's life and justly assess his accomplishments is through a reflection upon the ethics and politics of hero-celebration. This context permits us to examine the beneficial and harmful uses to which the King Holiday may be put in creating or preserving images of King that avoid disturbing history or dodge painful truth. This context also provides a healthy framework in addressing recent revelations about King's character, including charges of plagiarism and womanizing. In this essay, I will examine some characteristics of heroism, exploring the ways it makes sense to call King a hero, treat two central tensions that arise in asserting that King's heroism is ambiguous, and briefly suggest that King's birthday is indeed worth celebrating.

In my brief examination of some characteristics of heroism, I do not intend to provide a theory of heroism, or trace its varied genealogy. Rather, I will discuss heroism within the limits of existing understandings of the concept and then seek to apply them to King in analyzing the effects of hero worship on the ideals for which he gave his life.

In his work on George Washington, cultural critic and historian Gary Wills reminds us that hero worship

> is a hard assignment for many people today — one they think they cannot fulfill, or should not. Hero worship is elitist. It reduces the science of history to mere biography, if not to anecdote. It suggests that individual talent is a more important force than large economic processes ... The attitude of many in our time is captured by Bertolt Brecht's Galileo, who says: "Unhappy the land that needs a hero."[1]

While Wills' larger point about the suspicion of many Americans toward hero worship may be valid, explaining the diminished field of activity over which heroism is spread, it is equally true that American hero worship is presently focused in two social spheres: competitive sports and the military.

Contemporary forms of American heroism are often displayed within the context of sports competition where individual or team exploits are lauded for embodying particular virtues, skills and mastery. For example, basketball heroes are often said to embody the virtues of rigorous habits of practice, expert skills of physical dexterity, and mastery of the overall complexity of their craft necessary to perform excellently and unselfishly in a team sport.

Military heroes, as well, figure prominently in the comparatively constricted sphere of heroism celebrated today. America's recent war in the Gulf shows how eager Americans are for clear embodiments of American values of national patriotism, personal valor and sacrifice for the common good. That Generals Norman Schwarzkopf and Colin Powell are instant heroes testifies to the peculiar hunger of many Americans for reassurance about the integrity and rightness of this country's values and ways of life.

Perhaps this last point clearly demonstrates a telling feature of heroism: it is intimately related to ideals felt to be worthy of support because they say something important about national self-identity. Part of the difficulty in deciding upon a genuine and truly national hero is connected to the increasing diversity of American culture. Because of the bewildering pluralization of perspectives about what it means to be an American, growing dispute about what goods are worthy of pursuit, strong disagreement about how to measure various forms of moral and social excellence, and the unraveling of a unified concept of the public good, the virtuous as well as the heroic is subject to radical revision and heated debate. Occasionally, however, a person or movement so decisively captures the nation's imagination that a variety of Americans come to believe that their truest selves and deepest beliefs are embodied in the vision and life of that figure or movement. Such was the case for many Americans in relation to Martin Luther King, Jr., and the civil rights movement.

The civil rights movement provided a social context, cultural framework and racial worldview for blacks and other similarly excluded Americans to argue for inclusion within the larger circle of privilege, rights and status from which they had been socially and legally barred. Civil rights leaders and activists built upon the symbol systems of black religion, the resonant traditions of radical protest within black culture, and a progressive understanding of liberal democracy in articulating demands for equality, justice and freedom. Because of this potent mix of elements, the civil rights movement had the advantage of appealing to specific values nourished within a black cultural cosmos, while linking them to the iconic structures, symbolic worldviews, and heroic values that undergirded much of American society. As symbolic representative of the civil rights movement, Martin Luther King, Jr., embodied the virtues of black religious culture, and black traditions of protest, as well as the best impulses of Western liberal democracy.

On the other hand, King wove into his rhetorical and strategic tapestry threads of prophetic religious utterance and radical social criticism that sorely tested the limits of liberal tolerance of forces of fundamental social challenge and transformation. The fact that some state and national politicans who represent the forces of stasis and regression that King opposed are now in part responsible for presiding over the public rituals to commemorate his memory only attests to the ambiguous character of the heroism King embodies.

King figures prominently in a distinct line of social prophets whose ideals can sometimes only be truly honored by their remaining, in significant measure, outside of the totemic processes of official acceptance that cloak their status as prophetic characters whose memory judges American moral practice. The ambiguity that surrounds King's memory is healthy because it creates suggestive tensions within the developing edifice of King worship, and draws attention to those troubling aspects of King's thought that have the potential to shatter the rigid constructions of official truth.

In reflecting upon the ambiguity of King's heroism, it will be helpful to discuss some characteristics of heroism and explore how King can be usefully understood as an American hero. A heroic figure undeniably possesses the ability to substantially alter and influence the course of events because of her mix of personal traits, skills, talents and visions. This definition, of course, rests on the distinction that Sidney Hook made between two types of persons who qualify as potential heroes. After defining the hero in history as "the individual to whom we can justifiably attribute preponderant influence in determining an issue or even whose consequences would have been profoundly different if he had not acted as he did," Hook describes the difference in "eventful" persons and "event-making" persons.[2]

> The *eventful* man in history is any man whose actions influenced subsequent developments along a quite different course than would have been followed if these actions had not been taken. The *event-making* man is an eventful man whose actions are the consequences of outstanding capacities of intelligence, will, and character rather than of accidents of position. This distinction tries to do justice to the general belief that a hero is great not merely in virtue of what he does but in virtue of what he is.[3]

By Hook's measure, King certainly qualifies as a geniune hero, as someone whose combination of talents, intelligence and vision considerably altered the course of events. This does not mean that King was the only person in the civil rights movement who possessed high degrees of intelligence, discipline and skill. Numerous participants in the civil rights movement exhibited extraordinary leadership ability and qualities, ranging from the ingenious strategic skills of Bayard Rustin, the penetrating philosophic skills of Bob Moses, the uncanny organizational skills and folk wisdom of Fannie Lou Hamer, and the creative nonviolent theory of James Lawson.[4] While others possessed sharper skills than King in particular areas, King possessed a unique ability to inspire masses and maintain the loyalty of an impressive host of talented men and women. Perhaps this was best expressed by Benjamin Mays when he wrote:

> It may be that only one man in ten million could have led the Montgomery boycott without that city exploding into one of the worst race riots in history ... If the Montgomery Improvement Assocation had chosen a person other than King to communicate the Negroes' grievances to the city fathers, Dr. King might have gone through life as a successful Baptist preacher and no more. His rare ability to lead and inspire the classes as well as the masses, in a crusade for social justice, might never have been called forth.[5]

Furthermore, it may be argued that the force of King's personality, intelligence and gifts helped create the conditions for social change in regard to race relations. King thus exhibited what Hook meant in a further clarification of the eventful versus the event-making person.

> The event-making man, on the other hand, finds a fork in the historical road, but he also helps, so to speak, to create it. He increases the odds of success for the alternative he chooses by virtue of the extraordinary qualities he brings to bear to realize it. At the very least, he must ... display exceptional qualities of leadership. It is the hero as event-making man who leaves the positive imprint of his personality upon history — an imprint that is still observable after he has disappeared from the scene.[6]

As Lerone Bennett observed, King's ability to create the conditions that led to social transformation was clearly demonstrated in Birmingham, Alabama, where it is widely believed that the civil rights movement gained its greatest symbolic victory because of a highly publicized clash with Sheriff Bull Connors's violent tactics to repel the civil rights demonstrators.

> No leader, of course, can create an event the time is not prepared for. But the genius of the great leader lies precisely in his apprehension of what the times require and in carrying through in the teeth of great opposition an act that changes the times. In Birmingham, King approached that kind of greatness, creating the occasion of the 'Negro Revolution' by an act almost everyone said was ill-timed and ill-chosen. Birmingham ... was *chosen*, not stumbled upon. It was created by a man who knew exactly what he wanted and how much he would probably have to pay to get it.[7]

King was certainly a figure who often precipitated change through conscious, decisive action.

The hero, particularly the one who advances an agenda of trenchant social criticism and sweeping ethical reform, also possesses the ability to create a situation in which it is untenable to remain unchanged or unchallenged by the hero's vision of how things should be. The hero, in short compass, forces us to make moral choices. As James Hannigan says:

> One thing that makes the hero's course a precarious one is that the very nature of the hero's role in history requires the more ordinary among us to make choices. It is not simply a matter for us of liking or disliking, of admiring or ignoring the hero. Rather, we are forced to choose for or against the hero, for or against the vision, or dream, or message, or course of action the hero proposes to us. One hallmark of the hero's authenticity as a hero is precisely that he or she forces us to choose; we cannot remain indifferent to this presence among us, even if we would. For not to be with the hero is automatically to be against him or her.[8]

This aspect of heroism was quite evident in King's life. He constantly envisioned America as a work in progress, a nation constructed by the redemptive or destructive choices it would make about its moral and social future. In this regard, King was quintessentially American, placing the notion of experiment and pragmatic moral revisionism at the heart of his creed of American social life.

The primary impact of King's life and career may consist in the clarity he brought to the choices that Americans must make in "living out" the principal ideals of the American creed, particulary as embodied in the Constitution and the Declaration of Independence. King's genius and heroic stature derived from his adroit skill at pointing out the disintegration of the American Dream, and dramatically portraying the distance between American ideals of justice and equality, and its contradictory anti-democratic practices. But it was his willingness to die for American ideals that made King so dangerous, because he forced America to examine itself with the instruments of equality, justice and social morality America claimed as its own. Because of this quality in King's leadership, we may concede that "the possibility for heroism in our time will be tempered by the ideals we propose to ourselves — a thing proved in the heroic age of civil rights, when Dr. King and many others suffered and died for the concept of equality we profess but have not lived up to."[9]

Moreover, King's martyrdom also linked him to other American heroic figures, like Abraham Lincoln, and John and Robert Kennedy, whose deaths made them the subjects of national memory through eulogies and memorials, and gained them even greater status as the vehicles of American moral and social redemption. As Conrad Cherry perceptively notes in writing about Robert Kennedy's funeral, and by extension other funerals of national significance:

> In this funeral Americans joined in a sacred ceremony, the scope of which crossed denominational religious boundaries. Many citizens had participated in another such ceremony only a few weeks earlier at the funeral for Dr. Martin Luther King, Jr., and in still another only a few short years earlier at the funeral for President John F. Kennedy. American history is, in fact, replete with leaders who have been canonized in the national consciousness as exemplars of American ideals and as particular bearers of America's destiny under God. When those leaders have met their deaths they have become, in the national memory as well as in the ceremonies and speeches that surround their deaths, martyrs for the American cause, even in some cases redeemers.[10]

Equally important, heroism often enables ordinary people to make a critical difference in their social and personal existence by linking their lives to larger social goals and movements that embody the virtues to which they aspire. The ideals of equality, justice and freedom had for so long been uttered in public discourse and written in the creeds of American society, and had in varying degrees been realized for particular segments of American culture. But freedom, equality and justice often remained unrealized for many others, and King both envisioned how these ideals could be enfleshed, and boldly envisioned how enormous obstacles to their realization could be overcome. In this scenario, the individual hero functions as an enabler for a group of people to rise above their limiting circumstances and participate in a drama of redemption, reconstruction or transformation in which their roles, however small, are perceived as necessary and vital. Thus I will speak of this further when I discuss King's means of nonviolent transformation.

But the hero also looks to the group for insight and inspiration. Indeed, the group often serves a heroic function itself, engaging in which Max Weber called social heroism.

> Max Weber claimed that the Reformation and the attendant rise of capitalism were the last examples of middle class heroism. He is not alluding by this to the highly individualized gallantry of a John Wayne. Heroism for Weber is a social act. It occurs when a group of people no longer simply stand up for the system, but stand out against it. They critique the present and act to reclaim control over the future. The bourgeoisie of the Reformation era changed the circumstances of their existence and freed themselves from the dominance of aristocratic, social, political and economic structures.[11]

In this scenario, the hero often functions to recall great past deeds as the basis for present and future action by masses of people. King understood this, and acted on it.

But the prospect of King's heroism becomes more problematic as we reflect on why he is presently being officially canonized, while near the end of his life he was roundly dismissed as a hopeless romantic and an irrelevant idealist. What was the real nature of King's achievements? In this section, I want to explore the nature of King's genius, and then proceed to address two tensions which further reinforce the ambiguity of King's heroism. Although King possessed many gifts, I think his genius lay in his moral vision, and the choice of nonviolent means in attempting to achieve equality and real democracy for black Americans.

The idea that Martin Luther King was a man of moral vision raises questions about the nature of moral arguments, the particular content of moral statements, and the proper adjudication of competing moral claims. In our day, simply put, morality has fallen on hard times. This difficulty, though, does not absolve us of the responsibility to engage our every energy and resource in clarifying what we mean by morality and advancing a moral vision. King was willing, and able, to perform such a task. In fact, the historical conditions under which he and his comrades labored elicited from King and the civil rights movement a moral vision to guide and regulate its tasks and purposes.

Although King's moral vision may be variously conceived, I think, for my present purposes, it may be helpfully viewed in the following two ways. First, King's moral vision was not the work of one man. It expressed the hopes and aspirations of a long tradition of confrontation with and critical reflection upon the existential and social circumstances of black people in America. King did not invent or discover, but rather inherited, the imperative to rectify the evils of racism and impoverishment embedded in the legal, social, political, economic and religious structures of American society.

King was the son, grandson and great-grandson of Baptist preachers, so the very texture of his life from birth was religious and spiritual. He was reared under the powerful preaching of his father, the Rev. Martin Luther King, Sr., pastor of the Ebeneezer Baptist Church of Atlanta, Georgia. Martin Luther King, Jr. attended Morehouse College and came under the influence of, among others, the late Dr. Benjamin Elijah Mays, president of Morehouse and Dr. George Kelsey, who is now professor-emeritus at Drew University. These men, both scholar/preachers, provides for King the paradigm of ministry as an intellectually respectable, socially engaged and emotionally satisfying vocation. At nineteen Martin was ordained to the ministry and became associate pastor of Ebeneezer, and later its co-pastor, after serving six years as the pastor of Dexter Avenue Baptist Church in Montgomery, Alabama.

Given this background, King was firmly rooted in the institution that lies at the heart of Afro-American life, the black church. Throughout their history religion has been and remains the central ordering influence upon the vast majority of Americans of African descent. Albert Raboteau, in his ground-breaking work on the religion of Afro-American slaves, entitled *Slave Religion*, writes:

> ... black religious institutions have been the foundation of Afro-American culture. An agency of social control, a source of economic cooperation, an arena for political activity, a sponsor of education, and a refuge in a hostile white world, the black church has been historically the social center of Afro-American life.[12]

From its inception the black church identified racism (whether embedded in vicious slavery or embodied in white Christianity's segregationist ethos) as a heinous sin, and resolved to make its extirpation a primary goal of the black church's existence. The black church message that all people are children of God, and that everyone deserves to be treated with decency and respect found ample application in King's moral vision. The notion in the black church that God sides with the oppressed, as God sided with Israel against Egyptian bondage, inspired King's actions and was a central part of his moral vision as reflected in his belief that Afro-Americans had "cosmic companionship" in the struggle for liberation.

The Afro-American religious notion of loving and praying for one's enemies, despite their decadence, hate or brutality, had a strong affinity with the Gandhian philosophy of non-violence as a teaching, technique and lifestyle that King ardently preached and assiduously practiced. The black church understanding that all people, regardless of social standing, educational attainment, political sophistication or cultural refinement, are equal heirs to God's promises, found expression in King's concept of the beloved community where black and white, rich and poor, and powerful and powerless would be united in peace and harmony.

In these and many more significant ways was King organically linked to the living tradition of Afro-American religion. One aspect of King's genius was his ability to project this profoundly Afro-American religious sensibility into the American socio-political ethos and employ it as a base from which to argue for and, to a degree, affect social, political and economic transformation.

This ability reflects the second characteristic of King's moral vision: it countered the narrow exclusivism of a vulgar patriotism and put forward a creative reinterpretation of America's central political concepts and documents. King's moral hermeneutic understood these concepts generally in relation to American moral improvement, and specifically in relation to Afro-American freedom and liberation. In short, King appealed to the very documents that are central to American civil life, (the Constitution, Declaration of Independence), and pointed out their basis for a moral understanding and interpretation of concepts like equality, justice and freedom. Furthermore, he employed these documents as a yardstick to judge the actual attainment by American society of the goals, norms and ideals they articulated.

Not only, then, does King's moral vision have a religious moment, but it extends itself into the national civic realm, constituting its political moment.

King's moral vision was predicated upon, in part, what he understood to be the best in American religious, civil, legal, social and political history. He deemed his moral vision to be commensurate with American historic and national goals set forth in the Constitution and the Declaration of Independence, which help regulate American ideas about issues like freedom, justice and equality.

In fact, in his famous "I Have A Dream" speech, King clearly stated that his dream was "deeply rooted in the American dream."[11] When King confronted the massive and abusive legal, social and political structures which thwarted the materialization of Afro-American freedom, justice and equality in any concrete sense, he appealed to these documents in calling for the realization of norms and ideals they espoused. King said in Washington:

> I have a dream that one day this nation will rise up and live out the true meaning of its creed, 'We hold these truths to be self-evident that all men are created equal.'[12]

King believed, despite the fact that black people were slaves when this creed was written, that any fair-minded interpreter would be bound to enlarge its vision of liberty and equality to include all people. The principles articulated in the Constitution and the Declaration of Independence struck an authentic chord of truth for King that could not be nullified even by the shortsightedness of their original authors in regard to people of color. These documents provided a substantial foundation for American society to accord all people the status of persons with rights. King stated:

> When the architects of our Republic wrote the magnificent words of the Constitution and the Declaration of Independence, they were signing a promissory note to which every American was to fall heir. This note was the promise that all men, yes black men as well as white men, would be guaranteed the unalienable rights of life, liberty and the pursuit of happiness.[13]

King refused to permit the interpretation of democracy, liberty, justice and freedom to be monopolized by those who would truncate and distort the understanding of American history and ideals. King refused to allow either the overt barbarity of bigoted segregationists like the Ku Klux Klan and the White Citizens Council, or the covert but no less pernicious racism of prejudiced politicians, to define democracy. On the rhetorical battleground of American public ideology King wrested from them the prerogative of describing and defining what is authentically American, and in the process transformed the terms of American political and civil discourse. Martin Kuther King, Jr.'s moral vision, then, which was rooted in Afro-American religion and which advanced a creative American moral hermeneutic, was a powerful and often persuasive means for structuring a protest movement to secure basic rights for black Americans.

Another way of accounting for King's heroic character and genius is his insistence of militant nonviolence as the means of obtaining freedom, justice and equality for black people. King's advocacy of militant non-violence was important for two interrelated reasons. First, it appealed to the African-American religious heritage of black culture, while linking that heritage to other powerful models of resistance and social transformation. Second, it presumed the heroic character of everyday black folk to resist evil and located transformative agency within their grasp.

King's advocacy of non-violence was deeply anchored in an African-American religious ethic of love that promoted the fundamental dignity of all creatures because of their relationship to a loving, all-powerful God. As I have already indicated, norms and values developed in the black church influenced King's theological ideals, but they also shaped his strategies of social reform, and his beliefs about human potential for progress and change. What is crucial for the African-American religious ethic of love in relation to nonviolent means to attain social, economic and political freedom is that in King's world-view, nonviolence was a *way of life* and not simply a strategy of social transformation.

This distinction is key to understanding how King maintained a consistent moral stance toward various forms of violence, including war and domestic policies that reinforced poverty and classism. King saw nonviolent resistance to oppressive social structures, policies and persons as a means of acquiring basic necessities such as food, clothing and shelter, as well as being the only viable and ethically legitimate way to obtain freedom, justice and equality. Although the destruction of racism was a major goal of African-American nonviolent resistance, it was only one goal of the nonviolent lifestyle. As King matured politically, he began to expand his field of moral vision to include classism, proverty and militarism as legitimate object of social protest. He believed that conceiving of nonviolence as both a lifestyle and a means of resisting a variety of social and moral problems was consonant with the affirmation of life, liberty and equality in the black religious experience.

But King's advocacy of nonviolence was also the result of disciplined study of its applications in a variety of national, social and moral contexts. He examined the principled resistance to tax-paying advocated by Henry David Thoreau, as well as his seminal essay of civil disobedience. It is widely known that King also diligently studied the principles, methods and lifestyle of Mohandas Gandhi, whose "experiments with truth" had a powerful impact on King's thinking. Gandhi's leadership of millions of Indians to resist the systemic social oppression of British colonialism inspired King to adapt Gandhi's methods of nonviolent resistance to American society.

Second, King's advocacy of nonviolence presumed the heroic character of everyday black people. Although this presumption contained romantic notions of black self-identity, it also located forms of transformative agency within the grasp of often powerless ordinary black folk. It is important to remember that at the beginning of the civil rights movement the lot of everyday black people remained even more circumscribed by the forces of segregation, race hatred, and class inequality from which the black middle class had only occasionally, and precariously escaped. The civil rights movement provided an enormous boost to the self-identity of black people who had long believed that they were relatively powerless to change their condition.

However, Cornel West points out that King's presumption that black people could wield nonviolence as a means to social liberation contained a romantic notion of superiority over other racial groups, particularly white Americans. West also contends that King's doctrine of nonviolence

> tends to assume tacitly that Afro-Americans have acquired, as a result of their historical experience, a peculiar capacity to love their enemies, to endure patiently suffering, pain, and hardship and thereby 'teach the white man how to love' or 'cure the white man of his sickness.' King seemed to believe that Afro-Americans possess a unique proclivity for nonviolence, more so than do other racial groups, that they have a certain bent toward humility, meekness, and forbearance, hence are quite naturally disposed toward nonviolent action. In King's broad overview, God is utilizing Afro-Americans — this community of caritas (other-directed love) — to bring about ' the blessed community' . . . The self-image fostered. . . is defensive in character and romantic in content.[14]

While I think West's assessment is just, there is another dimension to King's assumption that must not be overlooked: his belief in the moral heroism of black people also assumed that the power to affect their destiny and to exercise transformative moral agency, was achievable by ordinary black folk. Like that of Marcus Garvey before him, and Malcolm X during his own day, the genius of King resided in the ability to appeal to his followers' heroic potentials by placing strict demands on their shoulders, challenging them to live up to a standard of moral excellence that neither they nor their opponents realized they possessed. King believed that black people could muster the resources they already had at their disposal, such as moral authority and limited by significant economic base, to foster legitimate claims to social goods like education, housing, and enfranchisement.

Moreover, the standards of moral excellence that King expected through disciplined participation in nonviolent demonstrations, which included rites of self-examination and purification, were of inestimable worth not only in fighting for denied social privileges and rights, but in the healthy enlargement of crucial narratives of racial self-esteem. King understood the virtues of everyday forms of resistance, and appealed to the weapons of the weak in opposing unjust social forces.

While the above discussion specifies how it makes sense to call King a hero, now I want to explore two tensions that flow from the assertion of King's ambiguous heroism which may be summed up in the following way: while King's contributions were heroic and significant, many African-Americans, particularly the working poor and the ghetto poor, still suffer in important ways; and while King deserves great honor and praise of a particular sort, he is indebted to traditions of African-American religious protest, social criticism and progressive democracy.

It must be conceded that despite the significant basic changes that King helped bring about, the present status of poor black Americans in particular presents little cause for celebration. Their situation does not mean that King's achievements were not substantial. Rather it reflects the deep structures of persistent racism and classism that have not yet yielded to sustained levels of protest and resistance.

In order to judge King's career, we must imagine what American society would be for blacks without his historic achievements. Without basic rights to vote, desegrated public transportation and accomodations, equal housing legislation, and the like, American society would more radically reflect what Gunnar Myrdal termed the American Dilemma. King and other participants in the civil rights movement wrought heroic change, but that change was a partial movement toward real liberation.

If it was once believed that King's vision was only a beginning, a mere foot in the door of civil rights, political empowerment, and economic equality, the tragic reality now is that the door has been shut fast in the face of many Afro-Americans. This is displayed particularly in two areas the persistence of racism, and the disintegration of postindustrial urban life.

It is fair to say that a climate of hostility has been generated toward those who assert that this country has not achieved the ideals of freedom, justice and equality in any significant structural manner, as envisioned by the mature Martin Luther King. The early Martin Luther King, Jr. was preoccupied with securing inclusion in American society as it is, without questioning the means by which wealth is distributed, without probing the mechanisms that determine privilege, prestige and status, and without challenging the growing classism that shattered the notion of monolithic black community.

The mature Martin Luther King, Jr. however, understood that economic injustice was just as great an impediment to black liberation as racial unjustice. As I will show later, King's mature career was spent in attempting to draw out the implications of a coalition politics that transcended race to speak of economic injustice and class oppression. His Poor People's March was the first real attempt to enact a coalition politics that bound together the interests of various marginalized groups, including Latinos, poor blacks and whites, and peace activitists.

Part of King's great frustration resulted from the fact that racism was much more complex and multifaceted than he realized at the beginning of his career, and he sought to educate himself and his colleagues about the stuctural nature of class oppresion. This accounts in part for how we can claim that King's contributions were heroic while acknowledging that they were neither perfect, nor permanent. Some of the gains King helped secure were structurally permanent, such as legally desegregated public housing and transportation. Other gains must be renegotiated through legislation. Moreover, the logic of racial progress is subject to perennial reexamination and justification.

The project to make King a particular sort of hero has often presented a picture of completion and satisfaction with regard to the structural obstacles to

African-American racial progress. However a suggestive and subversive side of King's heroism views him as an iconic figure who inspires continued battle to implement the goals and dreams for which he gave his life. It is consistent to suggest that although the general perception of blacks has changed, the actual legal barriers to social mobility have been removed, and particular categories of blacks have made substantial gains economically, King's life equally symbolizes the continued battle for the truly disadvantaged, the ghetto poor. It is heroic in a distinctly Kingian sense to resist official efforts at King canonization that both whitewash actual racial history and deny the work that remains, and to support the belief that much more progress must be made before real liberation can be achieved.

To suggest this, however, is to counter the self-image of the reigning political view of things that is the framework of contemporary conservative and liberal American socio-political ideology. Conservative political thought as construed here maintains that the struggle for black self-determination is largely over, and that suffficient energy has been devoted to the eradication of racism in American life. Liberal political thought even when it acknowledges the continuing expression of certain forms of racial and economic inequality, rarely effectively examines the reasons for their malignant persistence.

The predominant political ideology shrinks space for radical dissent and marginalizes, absorbs or excludes voices asserting that the American condition is in terrible disarray. In short, the ideological horizon and socio-political landscape have been dominated by conservative and liberal visions that constitute political realism, effectively preventing radical alternatives to their oftentimes mundane and pedestrian achievements.

Conservative ideology and politics have the effect of both offering limited and narrowly conceived options to Afro-American suffering, and ensuring the continued hegemony of white, upper middle class politics. Liberal alternatives, while certainly an improvement, are nevertheless plagued by an inability to move beyond a provincial vision of what economic and political measures are necessary to better Afro-American life. Liberalism attends to symptoms rather than root causes.

The tragic reality of the Afro-American condition is that, while in many respects blacks are certainly better off, in other respects many blacks continue to suffer. For instance the disintegration of the moral, economic and civic fabric of poor black communities is stunning and entails lethal social consequences. The arising of a subculture of crime, which thrives on the political economy of crack, is threatening to destroy the inner city. Also the gentrification of black urban living space means that inner city residents are being squeezed out of marginal neighborhoods by an escalating tax rate that forces the working poor into even poorer neighborhoods.

Poverty, for example, affects black people in an especially pernicious manner. Since the 1970's, there has been an enormous increase in poverty in America. In 1970, 14.9 percent of all children were poor. Today the figure is almost 21 percent. For minorities, it is even worse. Two out of every five

Hispanic children are poor, and almost one out of every two black children is poor. For black children under six, the poverty rate is a record high 51.1 percent. There is a continually widening gap between the wealthy and the poor in America, and this year it is the highest ever since the Census Bureau began collecting statistics in 1947. Last year, two-fifths of the population received 67 percent of all national income, the highest ever recorded. The poorest two-fifths, on the other hand, received only 15.7 percent of all income, the lowest ever recorded. Even worse, one-third of all black America remains below the poverty line.[15]

Another factor that has contributed to the current condition of black America for the better part of the eighties is the legacy of the Reagan era. The Reagan administation symbolized, and ominously expressed, a new breed of racism, generating policies pervaded by subtle forms of discrimination and prejudice that have had a devastating impact on black America. The Reagan administration's laissez-faire attitude toward the enforcement of laws and governmental policies that protect minorities, and its outright attack on the hard won rights of America's poor and dispossessed, helped set the tone for an almost unmitigated viciousness toward these groups.[16] The Reagan years have fueled a subversive shift in the modus operandi of American racism. Often no longer able to openly express racial hatred through barbaric deeds, racists have found subtle and insidious forms of expression.

This racisim not only is evident in upper middle class America with its staunchly conservative values and sensibilities that problematize Afro-American progress; and in the white working and underclass with its tightly turfed communities that cling to racial and ethnic identification as a means of exclusion and survival (e.g., Howard Beach and Bensonhurst).[17] But it also has in a cruelly ironic twist, engendered a new reactionary group of black neo-conservative political and intellectual figures. This group rejects civil rights as a means to black progress and naively contends that such measures as affirmative action cripple rather than aid black freedom by creating negative sterotypes about inferior black performance in education and employment. All of this suggests the deep dimensions of our current crisis.

The second tension in regard to King's heroism rests on the fact that although his achievements merit praise and honor, those accomplishments are related to a larger tradition of African-American protest, as well as traditions of liberal democracy. For instance, the King holiday reminds us that by celebrating King's life and career in particular, America celebrates the profound accomplishments of black America in general. This recognition offers to American intellectual life the vital resources of a living Afro-American intellectual tradition that can continue to inform, challenge, and even transform American discourse about race, class, justice, freedom and equality. More specifically, since, as I have stated above, King's life was developed and shaped in the ethos of a black church worldview; and since the *locus classicus* of his moral vision was the Afro-American religious experience, our attention is redirected back to that experience as a crucial resource for the maintenance and extension of King's moral vision, in alliance with other progressive socio-political, historical and economic thought.

Indeed, the notion that King himself was the producer, not the product, and the cause, not the effect, of Afro-American liberation potentials that had been long latent, and at times vitally visible, in the fabric of our national experience is entirely alien to King's thought. Although he believed historical forces, under the direction of a demanding but loving providence, had arranged his ascension to a leadership position, he always believed that he articulated what many black people thought, knew, and held to be true. King obviously understood that he was the voice for a protest movement that had been growing for a long while and that had finally gathered the strength to resist the cumulative evils visited upon black people by the apartheid like conditions in the American South. In fact, in speaking about the experience that initially catapulted him into international fame, King wrote:

> When I went to Montgomery, Alabama, as a pastor in 1954, I had not the slightest idea that I would later become involved in a crisis in which nonviolent resistance would be applicable. After I had lived in the community about a year, the bus boycott began. The negro people of Montgomery, exhausted by the humiliating experiences that they had constantly faced on the buses, expressed in a massive act of noncooperation their determination to be free. They came to see that it was ultimatley more honorable to walk the streets in dignity than ride the buses in humiliation. At the beginning of the protest the people called on me to serve as their spokesman.[18]

The recognition that King was part of a larger tradition disallows America to escape its obligation to those King represented by relegating his thought to the fixed and static past. Instead, it forces America to critically engage and constantly examine the dynamic contemporary expressions of the thought and practices emerging from the tradition that birthed and buttressed King.

Furthermore, the need for a reinvigorated moral vision can only be immediately strengthened by portraying the explicit relationship among King, the civil rights movement and the most recent and powerful popular expression of the Afro-American intellectual and religious tradition: the Jackson campaigns for president. No honest and complete assessment of the movements and forces made possible by King and his comrades, achievements can be performed without mention of the Jackson candidacy. The Jackson campaigns, which have already in a fundamental way transformed the shape and contours of modern American politics, were made possible by a host of historical ingredients, not the least of which was the tradition of socio-political insurgency stimulated by the Afro-American religious tradition and the civil rights movement.

The Jackson campaigns in part enact a profound transformation in the ideas we inherit from the mature Martin Luther King. They underscore the need for a transition from an initial emphasis on civil rights to an appreciation of issues of class, and economic inequality.[19] Thus the relationship between King and Jackson, as participants in the same tradition, and in active pursuit of the goals of economic empowerment, racial harmony, and universal justice, regulated by a vision developed in an Afro-American religious perspective, must not be lost as we celebrate King's birthday.

Indeed, as we celebrate his birthday we must exercise extreme caution in retrieving images of King, especially those that avoid the painful truth of recent revelations about King's character. The latter includes charges that King plagiarized portions of his dissertation, that he was a womanizer, and that he possibly physically abused a woman the night before his death. In the face of these revelations, how can we proceed celebrating King's life?

First, it is important to remember that the celebration of King's achievments is not predicated upon a notion of human perfection. Before these revelations, it was well known that King was a great but flawed human being. He admitted on several occasions his own guilt over sexual indiscretions, and pledged to remedy his infidelity with all strength to resist temptation that lay in him. King's obvious recognition of his finitude and limitation serves as a worthy model of emulation for us as we seek to celebrate his moral legacy of protest for civil and social rights. But his legacy of self-examination, admission of fault, and the attempt to concretely rectify the wrong, even if it is not always successfully done, is a model we can usefully incorporate as responsible and mature moral agents.

Second, the charges of King's alleged plagiarism are disturbing and inexcusable. To use someone else's written work without proper recitation is akin to a form of verbal thievery. This painful truth, however, forces us to raise even more questions about why it occurred. Since we cannot question King, we can only surmise, infer and speculate. King's dissertation was completed while he was pastoring his first church in Montgomery and during the beginning of the Montogomery bus boycott. Undoubtedly, the pressures of the burgeoning movement tempted King to plagiarize Jack Boozer's dissertation in order to complete his own doctoral studies.

Moreover, although many black scholars had passed through Boston University's doctoral program in religion, one peculiar and tragic legacy of racism involved the pernicious self-doubts that could have plagued any developing black scholar. Qualities of self-worth, competence, talent and skill are not developed in a vacuum, but are in part socially constructed and reproduced. In the mid fifties it is certainly conceivable that a young talented black doctoral student who was uncertain of his real worth, despite the encouragement of professors and colleagues, and who was faced with an unpredictable and unfolding social crisis, could be tempted to rely on work that had already been accepted and viewed as competent.

The best approach to these charges, as well as charges about King's possible physical abuse, can be made by developing a healthy and realistic framework of assessment of King's life and career that will remain consistent even in the event of other revelations about his person and character. The power of King's achievements, the real force of his genius, consisted in his passion for justice to be done for the most lowly and oppressed inhabitants of American society. His moral authority as a spokesperson for truth, equality and the embodiment of a particular slant on the American Dream cannot be compromised by revelations about his personal and student life.

What these revelations do achieve, however, is a sad reminder of the forces of wrong and dishonor by which we are all subject to be tempted and corrupted. King serves as a reminder that no figure establishes an Archimedean point of moral perfection from which to argue for social change, that all argument for transformation is immanent criticism rooted in the faults and limitations of being human, but those limitations do not ultimately destroy the truth for which limited and faulty humans stand. Althought the vehicle for that truth is tarnished, enough of the truth's power and persuasion can emerge to convince others of its necessity and worth. We must view King in such a realistic fashion. These revelations show that King was an enormously complex human being, confirming what we know of him as we study his ideological evolutions and his political maturation.

As has been much remarked on, toward the end of his life King began to discern inadequacies in his former analyses of racial antipathy, social injustice and economic inequality. He discovered that these problems were much more deeply rooted and structurally expressed than he had initially surmised.

As a result he focused his considerable critical skills on the larger national and international economic, political and social contexts of Afro-Americans', and other oppressed people's, plight. King began to speak about the redistribution of resources, guaranteed incomes for the poor and forming a multi-racial coalition of the unemployed and the poor. This signified his changing perspective. In an article written just before his assassination and published after it, King wrote:

> We call our demonstration a campaign for jobs and income because we feel that the economic question is the most crucial that black people, and poor people generally, are confronting. . . We need an economic bill of rights. This would guarantee a job to all people who want to work and are able to work. It would also guarantee an income for all who are not able to work. . .I hope that a specific number of jobs is set forth, that a program will emerge to abolish unemployment, and that there will be another program to supplement the income of those whose earnings are below the poverty level.[20]

King had already begun to speak out against the war in Vietnam, decrying the lamentable manner in which resources for the poor were being pilfered by an ever-increasing war chest. He was criticized within the civil rights movement for squandering its social influence and political capital with the Johnson Administration. He was attacked outside the movement for delving, even "meddling," into larger domestic and foreign affairs that were not the legitimate concern of a civil rights leader.

Kings' moral vision, however, could not abide the spurious schizophrenia that compartmentalized moral concern into distinct and separable spheres. Morality was a piece to King, and his moral vision was integrated and unified.

The whole of life fell under its searching purview and rigorous scrutiny. King's later efforts to unite poor blacks, whites and other minorities, as well as labor and other progressive concerns, marked him as a highly dangerous man who was greatly feared in many governmental, political and social quarters.

These facts must be recalled as we engage in the rituals of remembrance and rites of recovery of the meaning of King's moral vision. We must refuse those who would commodify King's career into acceptable packages of comfortable, and not dangerous, memory, to be consumed by the American public in the name of a mythologization project intent on subverting King's radical and disturbing memory. In short, we must engage in hermeneutical combat and interpretive warfare over the future of King's memory, making certain that the custodians of the King canon include and remember his provocative words and oppositional ideas, as well as his comforting thoughts and hopeful beliefs.[21] Martin Luther King, Jr., was a man who possessed a profound moral vision that was rooted in the Afro-American religious experience, and that advanced a creative American moral hermeneutic. Remembering his life and thought challenges us to examine the present condition of American moral life and discover it wanting in regard to its treatment of those King represented: the black, the poor, and the oppressed.

Construed in the above manner, King's birthday serves as an outpost in progressive terrain, creating space in which to collect the energies of protest and struggle as they are related to the visionary revival and recovery of the moral tradition within which King lived and labored. King Day can facilitate a broadely conceived coalition of the oppressed and suffering who have a desperate interest in recovering the symbol and substance of King's moral vision.

Celebrating Martin Luther King's birthday as an official holiday promises a poignant and profound change in the rhythm of public rituals commemorating events of ultimate national and historical significance. King Day structures in the recurring cycle of American holidays a period of time that concentrates attention upon the meaning of King's life and thought. It also extends beyond King, transcending his personal and individual meaning, and celebrates the ingenuity of black survival in an American political, social and cultural ethos often inimical to Afro-American existence.

King Day also points us back to that Afro-American religious tradition that produced King, and that continues to thrive in the midst of American religious, social and political life. It also provides a means of reconstituting King's moral vision by challenging us each year to more closely approximate in our national and individual life and thought the goals and purposes for which he gave his life. In this sense, the name Martin Luther King, Jr., no longer merely represents the time and place of his life and body on earth, but symbolizes the hope of oppressed people everywhere that the dignity and worth of human life will be universally respected and uplifted.

Notes

1. Gary Wills, *Cincinnatus: George Washington and The Enlightenment* (Garden City: Doubleday & Company, Inc.), p. 109.
2. Sidney Hook, *The Hero In History: A Study in Limitation and Possibility* (New York: The John Day Company), p. 153.
3. Ibid., p. 154.
4. For a good social characterization of the figures who surrounded King in the civil rights movement, see Taylor Branch's commanding social history, *Parting The Waters: America in the King Years, 1955-1963*, Simon and Schuster, 1989.
5. This quote is from Benjamin Mays' introduction Lerone Bennett's *What Manner of Man: A Biography of Martin Luther King, Jr.* (Chicago: Johnson Publishing Company, Inc.), p. ii.
6. Hook, *The Hero in History*, p. 157.
7. Bennett, *What Manner of Man*, p. 131.
8. James P. Hannigan, *Martin Luther King, Jr. And The Foundations of Nonviolence*, (New York: Univeristy Press of America) pp. 31-2.
9. Wills, *Cincinnatus*, p. 132.
10. Conrad Cherry, *God's New Israel: Religious Interpretations of American Destiny*, (Englewood Cliffs: Prentice-Hall, Inc.,) p. 6.
11. Paul G. King, Kent Maynard, and David O. Woodyard, *Risking Liberation: Middle Class Powerlessness and Social Heroism* (Atlanta: John Knox Press), p. 15.
12. Albert J. Raboteau, *Slave Religion* (New York: Oxford University Press, 1978), p. iv.
11. Martin Luther King, Jr., "I Have A Dream," in James Melvin Washington, ed., *A Testament Of Hope: The Essential Writings of Martin Luther King, Jr.* (New York: Harper and Row, 1986), p. 219.
12. Ibid., p. 219.
13. Ibid., p. 217.
14. Cornel West, *Prophesy Deliverance: An Afro-American Revolutionary Christianity* (Philadelphia: Westminster), pp. 74-5.
15. These Census Bureau figures are usually reported on annually by Robert Greenstein in *Christianity and Crisis*. For a good example of such reporting, see John Bickerman and Robert Greenstein, "High and Dry on the Poverty Plateau," *Christianity and Crisis* (28 October, 1985), pp. 411-12.
16. For example, the Supreme Court is now, in effect, "Reagan's Court," due to Reagan's appointees, who legally enact his conservative political agenda. For commentary on how the Supreme Court has turned back the clock on affirmative action, see my "Deaffirmation," *Nation*, Volume 249, No. 1, July 3, 1989, pp. 4-5.
17. For a brief exploration of racism in both segments of society, see my article, "The Two Racisms," in *The Nation* (vol. 249, No. 1, July 3, 1989), pp. 4-5.
18. Washington, *Testament of Hope*, p. 38.
19. Roger Hatch describes the relation between the perspective of the mature Martin Luther King, Jr., and Jackson's vision for America, and addresses Jackson's evolution into the second phase of the civil rights movement, which concentrates on equity in every area of life (particularly economic justice), in *Beyond Opportunity: Jesse Jackson's Vision for America* (Philadelphia: Fortress Press, 1988), especially pp. 11-23.
20. Washington, *Testament of Hope*, pp. 67, 70.
21. I touch on this briefly in my short essay reflecting on the meaning of King and his death twenty years after his assassination, in, "Martin's Death, And Ours?" *Theology Today*, Vol. XLV, No. 1, April, 1988, pp. 68-70.

X

'Eid al-Adha (Feast of Sacrifice) in Islam: Abraham, Hagar and Ishmael

BY RIFFAT HASSAN

The deepest truths and insights which lie at the heart of each major religious tradition are, oftentimes, represented by means of myth and symbol which are able to inform, form and transform the inner and outer lives of millions of human beings through the ages. By commemorating such myth and symbol we not only celebrate the pivotal role they have played in our lives, as individuals or communites, in the past, but also reflect on ways in which they may be relevant to our lives in the present and the future. Today, as we meet in honor of the remembrance of what we consider to be of central import and significance in our religious traditions, I would like to focus on the 'Eid al-Adha, the Festival or Fest of Sacrifice, which is associated in the Islamic tradition with the story of Abraham as an emblem of the unity of all those who believe in the One God.

'Eid al-Adah is also called 'Eid al-qurban, 'Eid al-nahr or 'Eid al-kabir. In India it is commonly referred to as Bakar or Bakra 'Eid and in Turkey as Buyuk-Bairam or Qurban-Bairam.[1] 'Eid al-Adha is a festival which lasts for three days known as the "aiyam al-tashrik". It is celebrated on the 10th day of the Dhu'l-Hijja which is the 12th month of the Islamic calendar. On this day the pilgrims offer a sacrifice in the valley of Mina as the final rite of the Hajj which is one of the five pillars of faith for Muslims. The custom of offering a sacrifice on this day is followed not only by pilgrims but by all Muslims who regard it as sunnah or practical tradition of the Prophet Muhammad. This sunnah is regarded as obligatory on every free Muslim who has the means to buy a sacrificial animal. Amongst the animals sacrificed are sheep, goats, camels and cattle. The sacrificial animals should be of a fixed age and be free from certain physical defects (e.g. lame, one-eyed, etc.) The period of the sacrifice begins with the "salat al-'Eid" and ends with sunset on the third of the three aiyam al-tashrik.[2]

For those offering the sacrifice, the following practices are recommended:

1. The "tasmiya" or the saying of the "Bismillah" ("I begin in the name of Allah, Most Merciful, Most Compassionate.")
2. The "salat 'ala 'l-nabi" or the blessing on the Prophet.
3. The turning toward the "Qibla" in Mecca.
4. The three-fold "Takbir" ("Allah-O-Akbar") before and after the "tasmiya".
5. A prayer that Allah accept the sacrifice.[3]

If the sacrifice is made voluntarily as is generally the case, the person(s) offering the sacrifice may keep a portion (a third) of the sacrificed animal and give the rest away. However, if the sacrifice is made on account of a vow or a pledge ("nadr") all of it must be given away.[4]

The "salat al-'Eid" which is the festival of public prayer of the whole community is considered a sunnah. It consists only of two "rak'as"[5] and contains several takbirs more than the oridinary salat. After it a "khutba" (sermon) in two parts is held. It has no "adhan" (call to prayer) and no "ikama" (second call to prayer)[6]. The only summons to it is the words "al-salat jami'at an". It should be celebrated, if possible, in the open air on the "musalla" (place where the salat is performed on certain occasions).[7] The time for the performance is between sunrise and the moment when the sun has reached its zenith.[8]

The 'Eid al-Adha is the culmination of Hajj which comprises a number of rituals associated with the Prophet Abraham (Ibrahim), Hagar (Hajira) and Ishmael (Isma'il) who stand, according to the Islamic tradition, at the start of the new civilization in which Islam was to be born.

The founding of Mecca which enshrines the Ka'ba and is the birthplace of Islam is traced back in the Islamic tradition to Hagar who was left in an uninhabited place along with her infant son Ishmael. The story of what happened to Hagar has been graphically narrated in the *Sahih al-Bukhari*, the most authoritative Hadith-collection in Sunni Islam. The story of Hagar, not mentioned in the Qur'an, is given in considerable detail in *Sahih al-Bukhari* in a number of overlapping traditions in Book LV: *The Anbiya (Prophets)*, Chapter 9., Hadith number 583 mentions many significant features of the Hagar-Story as Muslims know it. Its earlier part (which refers to the death of "Ishmael's mother") reads as follows:

> Narrated Ibn 'Abbas: "The first lady to use a girdle was the mother of Ishmael. She used a girdle so that she might hide her tracks from Sarah.[9] Abraham brought her and her son Ishmael while she was suckling him, to a place near the Ka'ba under a tree on the spot of Zam-zam, at the highest place in the mosque. During

those days there was nobody in Mecca, nor was there any water. So he made them sit over there and placed near them a leather bag containing some dates, and a small water-skin containing some water, and set out homeward. Ishmael's mother followed him saying, 'O Abraham! Where are you going, leaving us in this valley where there is no person whose company we may enjoy, nor is there anything (to enjoy)?' She repeated that to him many times, but he did not look back at her. Then she asked him, 'Has Allah ordered you to do so?' He said, 'Yes!' She said, 'Then He will not neglect us," and returned while Abraham proceeded onwards, and on reaching Thaniya where they could not see him, he faced the Ka'ba, and raising both hands, invoked Allah saying the following prayers: 'O our Lord! I have made some of my offspring dwell in a valley without cultivation, by Your Sacred House (Ka'ba at Mecca) in order, O our Lord, that they may offer prayer perfectly. So fill some hearts among men with love towards them, and (O Allah) provide them with fruits, so that they may give thanks.' (Surah 14: *Ibrahim*: 37) Ishmael's mother went on suckling Ishmael and drinking from the water (she had). When the water in the water-skin had all been used up, she became thirsty and her child also became thirsty. She started looking at (Ishmael) tossing in agony: she left him, for she could not endure looking at him, and found that the mountain of Safa was the nearest mountain to her on that land. She stood on it and started looking at the valley keenly so that she might see somebody, but she could not see anybody. Then she descended from the Safa and when she reached the valley, she tucked up her robe and ran in the valley like a person in distress and trouble, till she crossed the valley and reached the Marwa mountain where she stood and started looking, expecting to see somebody but she could not see anybody. She repeated that (running between Safa and Marwa) seven times."

The Prophet said, "This is the source of the tradition of the walking of people between them (i.e., Safa and Marwa). When she reached the Marwa (for the last time) she heard a voice and she asked herself to be quiet and listened attentively. She heard the voice again and said, 'O, (whoever you may be!) You have made me hear your voice; have you got something to help me?' And behold! She saw an angel at the place of Zam-zam, digging the earth with his heel (or his wing), till water flowed from that place. She started to make something like a basin around it, using her hands in this way, and started filling her water-skin with water with her hands, and the water was flowing out after she had scooped some of it." The Prophet added, "May Allah bestow Mercy on Ishmael's mother! Had she let the Zam-zam (flow without trying to control it) (or had she not scooped from that water) (to fill her water-skin), Zam-zam would have been a stream flowing on the surface of the earth." The Prophet further added, "Then she drank (water) and suckled her child. The angel said to her, 'Don't be afraid of being neglected, for this is the house of Allah which will be built by this boy and his father, and Allah never neglects his people.' The house (i.e., Ka'ba) at that time was on a high place resembling a hillock, and when torrents came, they flowed to its right and left. She lived in that way till some people from the tribe of Jurhum passed by her and her child, as they (i.e., the Jurhum people) were coming through the way of Kada'. They landed in the lower part of Mecca where they saw a bird that had the habit of flying around water and not leaving it. They said, 'This bird must be flying around water, though we know that there is no water in this valley.' They sent one or two messengers who discovered the source of water. So they all came (towards the water)." The Prophet added, "Ishmael's mother was sitting near the water. They asked her, 'Do you allow us to stay with you?' She replied, 'Yes, but you will have no right to possess the water.' They agreed to do that." The Prophet further said, "Ishmael's mother was pleased with the whole situation as she used to love to enjoy the company of people. So, they settled there, and later on they sent for their families who came and settled with them so that some families became permanent residents there. The child (i.e., Ishmael) grew up and learnt Arabic from them and (his virtues) caused them to love and admire him as he grew up, and when he reached the age of puberty they made him marry a woman from amongst them. After Ishmael's mother had died, Abraham came after Ishmael's marriage in order to see his family that he had left before, but he did not find Ishmael there. . ."[9]

Although it may be inferred from the hadi*th* cited above that Sarah did not look kindly upon Hagar who was fearful of her, it is clear from the text that Abraham's decision to leave Hagar and Ishmael in the desert (believed by Muslims to be in the vicinity of Mecca) was not based upon his desire to appease his first wife. Abraham, while not disclosing to Hagar why he is leaving her and her infant son in the wilderness, does respond in the affirmative to her question whether God had commanded him to do so. Abraham's prayer, said when he is out of Hagar's sight, shows that he believes that in order to fulfil the prophetic mission of building the Sacred House of God (which Muslims believe to be the first House of God at Mecca) it was necessary to leave a part of his family in the uninhabited, uncultivated land. His prayer further indicates his faith that this uninhabited, uncultivated land will become populated and fruitful and that God will ensure that those whom he is leaving behind will find sustenance and love in their new environment.

While the Biblical narrative of *Genesis*, Chapter 21, 8-14, tends to leave readers with the impression that Abraham sent Hagar and Ishmael away in order to placate the jealous wrath of Sarah and had nothing more, henceforward, to do with them, the story as told in *Sahih Al-Bukhari* shows that Abraham had a continuing relationship with that part of his family. Muslims believe that Abraham returned periodically to visit Hagar and Ishmael. In the hadi*th* cited earlier, mention is made of a visit to Ishmael's family after the death of "Ishmael's mother."[10] That not only Hagar but also Sarah accepted what Abraham believed to be God's plan for his offspring is brought out in Hadi*th* Number 584[11] which is a variant of Hadi*th* Number 583. In this hadi*th* it is stated that each time Abraham thought of visiting Ishmael, he informed Sarah of his intentions.

The figure of Hagar which emerges from the traditions narrated in *Sahih Al-Bukhari* is that of a woman of exceptional faith, love, fortitude, resolution and strength of character. Once she hears from Abraham that it is God's command that she and her infant son should be left in the desert, she shows no hesitation whatever in accepting her extremely difficult situation. She does not wail or rage or beg Abraham not to abandon her and Ishmael. Instead, surrendering spontaneously and totally to what she believes to be Gods' will, she says that she is "satisfied to be with Allah" who will never neglect her. She lets Abraham go, without any words of recrimination or sorrow, and returns to her infant son. With a small supply of food and water, her major concern is to increase her milkflow so that she can feed her child adequately. Once out of water she knows that both their lives are imperilled. Unable to endure the sight of her baby son writhing in agony due to dehydration, she undertakes a massive search for help. Running frantically between Safa and Marwa she searches desperately for some sign of hope. Her refusal to give up, to keep running and looking and praying for help demonstrates her determination to fight for her beloved child's life to the last drop of her own strength. Finally, her faith and effort are rewarded and Archangel Gabriel appears to guide her to the spring Zam-zam (whose waters are believed by Muslims to have medicinal or miraculous powers) Through Zam-zam, Hagar is able not only to save her own and Ishmael's life, but also to attract the people of the tribe of Jurhum into becoming her companions and partners in creating a prosperous settlement.[12] She raises her son to become a God-conscious man, loved and admired for his many qualities, who becomes his father Abraham's chosen partner in building the first House of God in Mecca.

While Abraham is viewed by the Islamic tradition as the first "Muslim" or true believer in God, Hagar is viewed as the pioneer woman who led the way to the establishment of a new civilization. She is seen not only as "Ishmael's mother" but also as the mother of all Arabs and of those who later became the followers of the Prophet Muhammad, a descendant of the Prophet Ishmael. Hagar, a black slave-girl, rose from the lowest of positions to the highest place of honor in the Islamic tradition. (Here, it may be noted that in Muslim societies it is the mother who is the most highly revered member of the family since, following one — of the most popular traditions of the Prophet Muhammad, Muslims widely believe that Paradise lies under the feet of the mother). The dramatic story of her life shows that color or class are not a deterrent to any person — man or woman — who has faith in God and is resolutely righteous in action. Hagar, in the Islamic tradition, does not see herself as a victim of Abraham, Sarah, or a patriarchal, class-and-race-conscious culture. She is a victor who, with the help of God and her own initiative, is able to transform a wilderness into the cradle of a new world dedicated to the fulfillment of God's purpose on earth. Each year as millions of Muslim pilgrims run or walk between the points which symbolize Safa and Marwa they pay homage to Hagar who has become an indestructible emblem not only of a mother's love for her offspring but of a true believer's faith in the saving power of God. Hagar's shadow looms large over the valley where she once stood alone and her spirit is as inextricably embodied in the Ka'ba as that of her husband Abraham and her son Ishmael.

Finally, Hagar is associated, in the Islamic tradition, with the idea of "Hijrah", or going into exile for the sake of God. While in the Jewish tradition the idea of the diaspora, or the dispersion of the Jewish people in alien lands, inspires feelings of sorrow and nostalgia for a return to homeland and community, according to the Qur'an, the state of "Hijrah" is a blessed one. It is when one is in the wilderness, without the protection of any familiar framework or faces, that one's faith in God and oneself is put to a real test. Those who are willing to confront the challenge of "Hijrah", to leave their place of origin or sojourn in order to live in accordance with the will and pleasure of God, gain merit in the sight of God, as is indicated by many passages in the Qur'an.[13]

The Prophet Muhammad becomes a exemplar of "Hijrah" as he left his birthplace Mecca and chose to live in another city so that he could further his prophetic mission of establishing an Islamic society. In doing so he followed in the footsteps of his mother, Hagar, who generations earlier, had chosen to dwell in the desert to which God had directed her, making a home and community out of an unknown land and people. She demonstrated by her faith and actions that for a believer all of God's earth is a sanctified place, that loyalty to God supersedes attachment to terrestrial bonds, be they of place or persons.

Today, not only Muslim daughters of Hagar, but all women who are oppressed by systems of thought or structures based upon ideas of gender, class or race inequality, are called upon to be like her. They must have the faith and courage to venture out of the security of the known into the insecurity of the unknown, and to carve out, with their own hands, a new world from which the injustices and inequities which separate men from women, class from class, and race from race, have been eliminated.

While Hagar's story is recounted in the Hadi*th* literature, the symbolic significance of Abraham is underscored in a number of Qur'anic passages. It is important to understand how special Abraham is to Muslims. Not only is he the Prophet most often mentioned in the Qur'an after the prophet Muhammad, but he is also the one who broke away from polytheism to become the first "Muslim". The Qur'an repeatedly describes Abraham as "hanif" or one who turns away from all that is not-God to submit to God's law and order.[14] The Islamic tradition sees Abraham as a unifying figure whom all three Abrahamic traditions - Judaism, Christianity and Islam - can look back to and claim as their own. The prominence given to Abraham by the Qur'an and by the Islamic tradition is evident throughout the most significant as well as the most spectacular social ritual of the Muslim world: the "Hajj" or pilgrimage. The Qur'an portrays Abraham and his son Ishmael as builders of the Ka'ba and states that God had commanded Abraham to proclaim the first pilgrimage (Surah 21; *Al-Hajj*: 26-29). During the "Hajj", all pilgrims pray at the Station ("Maqam") of Abraham. Then there is commemoration and ritual enactment of the frantic search for water by Hagar as she ran seven times between the hills of Safa and Marwa. The appearance of the Zam Zam - to whose waters medicinal powers are attributed - is associated with the infant Ishmael beating the earth with his legs. The stoning of the devil and the sacrifice ceremony at the end of the "Hajj" is also associated with Abraham.

According to the Qur'an,[15] Abraham was one of God's chosen ones and blest both in this world and Hereafter:

2[130] And who turns away
From the religion of Abraham
But such as debase their souls
With folly? Him We chose
And rendered pure in this world;

And he will be in the Hereafter
In the ranks of the Righteous.
16[120] Abraham was indeed a model,
Devoutly obedient to God,
(And) "hanif", and he
Joined not gods with God:
121 He showed his gratitude
For the favors of God,
Who chose him, and guided him
To a Straight Way
122 And We gave him good
In this world, and he will be,
In the Hereafter, in the ranks
Of the Righteous.
29[27] And We have (Abraham)
Isaac and Jacob, and ordained
Among his progeny Prophethood
And Revelation, and We
Granted him his reward
In this life; and he was
In the Hereafter (of the company)
Of the Righteous.

The Qur'an refers to Abraham as the friend of God:

4[125] Who can be better
In religion than one
Who submits his whole self
To God, does good,
And follows the way
Of Abraham the "hanif"?
For God did take
Abraham for a friend.

Surah 37: *As-Saffat*: 83-4 point out that Abraham approached God with a heart and mind in total accord with the Will of the Creator and that God recognized and rewarded the faith of Abraham:

21[51] We bestowed aforetime
On Abraham his rectitude
Of conduct, and well were We
Acquainted with him.

38[45] And commemorate Our Servants
Abraham, Isaac, and Jacob
Possessors of Power and Vision.
46 Verily We did choose them
For a special (purpose)-
Proclaiming the Message
Of the Hereafter.
47 They were, in Our sight,
Truly, of the company
Of the Elect and the Good.

In his poetry, Muhammad Iqbal - modern Islam's most outstanding poet - philosopher, frequently pictures Abraham as an iconoclast who is shown breaking his father's idols. To Iqbal it is necessary to negate all that is not - God (signified by the "la" in the "la ilaha illa Allah": "There is no God but God" in the Islamic Shahadah or Confession of Faith) before God's existence can be affirmed. Iqbal's motif captures the spirit of the Qur'anic epithet "hanif" which refers not only to a belief in the One God but also a complete refusal to associate anything or anyone with God. Abraham is "hanif" precisely because he upheld the Oneness and Allness of God in the face of all opposition and obstacles:

2[135] They say, Become Jews
Or Christians if ye would be guided
(To salvation)" Say thou:
"Nay! (I would rather) the Religion
Of Abraham the 'hanif'
And he joined not gods with God."

3[95] Say: God speaketh
The Truth: follow
The religion of Abraham,
The "hanif" in faith; he
Was not of the Pagans.

6[161] Say: Verily, my Lord
Hath guided me to
A way that is straight, -
A religion of right, -
The path (trod) by Abraham
The "hanif"
And he (certainly)
Joined not gods with God.

16[123] So We have taught thee
The inspired (message),
Follow the ways of Abraham
The "hanif" and he
Joined not gods with God.

From the afore-cited Qur'anic passages it becomes evident that the prominence given to Abraham by the Islamic tradition is grounded in the very Revelation upon which Islam is founded. But though the Qur'an stresses the point that Abraham was "neither a Jew nor a Christian" (thus a symbol of unity rather than division), it also repeats with force and clarity that Islam is a confirmation and a continuation of the message given by God to all the Prophets before the time of Muhammad, for instance,

2[136] Say ye: We believe
In God, and the revelation
Given to us, and to Abraham,
Isma'il, Isaac, Jacob

And the Tribes, and that given
To (all) Prophets from their Lord:
We make no difference
Between one and another of them
And we bow to God (in Islam)

3[3] It is He Who sent down
To thee (step by step),
In truth, the Book.
Confirming what went before it;
And he sent down Law
(Of Moses) and the Gospel
(Of Jesus) before this,
As a guide to mankind,
And He sent down the Criterion
(Of judgment between right and wrong)

3[84] Say: We believe
In God, and in what
Has been revealed to us
And what was revealed
To Abraham, Isma'il,
Isaac, Jacob, and the Tribes
And in (theBooks)
Given to Moses, Jesus,
And the Prophets,
From their Lord:
We make no distinction
Between one and another
Among them, and to God to
Bow our will (in Islam).

4[163] We have sent thee
Inspiration as we have sent it
To Noah and the Messengers
After him: We sent
Inspiration to Abraham,
Isma'il, Isaac, Jacob
And the Tribes, to Jesus,
Job, Jonah, Aaron, and Solomon,
And to David We gave
The Psalms.

42[13] The same religion has He
Established for you as that
Which He enjoined on Noah -
That which We have sent
By inspiration to thee -
And that which We enjoined
On Abraham, Moses and Jesus:
Namely, that ye should remain
Steadfast in Religion, and make
No divisions therein:

To those who worship
Other things than God,
Hard is the (way)
To which thou callest them

In view of the linkage between Islam and the Hebrew Prophets, it is hardly surprising that the early Muslims prayed facing Jerusalem, the 'holy' city revered by both Jews and Christians. The Hijrah (migration) of the Prophet and the Muslims occurred in 622 A.D. and was followed by years of conflict and bitterness between Muslims and Jews in Medina. In 624 A.D., a Qur'anic revelation decreed that the direction of prayer be changed from Jerusalem to Mecca. A number of non-Muslim writers explain this change by saying that it was due to the growing tension between the Jews of Medina and Muhammad or that it was motivated by a desire to break away from the religious tie with the Jewish-Christian heritage and establish a national state. These explanations offend Muslims mainly because the underlying implication is that the Qur'an is not the Word of God but the work of Muhammad who at different times issued statements designed to meet different political needs or expediencies. From an Islamic standpoint any suggestion that Muhammad manipulated the Revelation in any way is tantamount to casting doubt upon the authenticity of the Islamic religious tradition in toto.

If one looks at the question of the change in Qibla from the point of view of a Muslim who accepts that the directive came not from Muhammad but from God, how is one to understand the reasons for and meaning of this change? An examination of the relevant Qur'anic passage is all-important and provides many significant insights:

2[142] The Fools among the people
Will say: "What hath turned
Them from the Qibla to which
They were used?" Say:
To God belong both East and West:
He guideth whom He will
To a Way that is straight.
143 Thus have We made of you
An Ummat justly balanced,
That ye might be witnesses
Over the nations,
And the Apostle a witness
Over yourselves;
And We appointed the Qibla
To which thou wast used,
Only to test those who followed
The Apostle from those
Who would turn on their heels
(From the Faith). Indeed it was
(A change) momentous, except
To those guided by God.
And never would God

Make your faith of no effect.
For God is to all people
Most surely full of kindness,
Most Merciful.
144 We see the turning
Of thy face (for guidance)
To the heavens: now
Shall We turn thee
To a Qibla that shall
Please thee. Turn then
Thy face in the direction
Of the sacred Mosque:
Wherever ye are, turn
Your faces in that direction.
The People of the Book
Know well that that is
The truth from their Lord.
Nor is God unmindful
Of what they do.
145 Even if thou went to bring
To the people of the Book
All the Signs (together),
They would not follow
Thy Qibla; nor art thou
Going to follow their Qibla;
Nor indeed will they follow
Each other's Qibla. If thou
After the knowledge hath reached thee,
Wert to follow their (vain)
Desires, - then wert thou
Indeed (clearly) in the wrong.
146 The people of the Book
Know this as they know
Their own sons; but some
Of them conceal the truth
Which they themselves know.
147 The Truth is from thy Lord;
So be not at all in doubt.

148 To each is a goal
To which God turns him;
Then strive together (as in a race)
Towards all that is good.
Wheresoever ye are,
God will bring you
Together. For God
Hath power over all things.

149 From whencesoever
Thou startest forth, turn
Thy face in the direction
Of the Sacred Mosque;
That is indeed the truth

From thy Lord. and God
Is not unmindful
Of what ye do.

150 So from whencesoever
Thou startest forth, turn
Thy face in the direction
Of the Sacred Mosque;
And wheresoever ye are,
Turn your face thither:
That there is no ground
Of dispute against you
Among the people,
Except those of them that are
Bent on wickedness; so fear
Them not, but fear Me;
And that I may complete
My favours on you, and ye
my (consent to) be guided;

151 A similar (favour)
Have ye already received
In that We have sent
Among you an Apostle
Of your own, rehearsing to you
Our Signs, and sanctifying
You, and instructing you
In Scripture and Wisdom,
And in new Knowledge.

As pointed out earlier, "Qibla" may be understood as the direction in which Muslims turn their faces when they pray and in this sense the afore-mentioned Qur'anic passage decrees a change in Qibla commanding Muslims to turn in the direction of the Sacred Mosque when they pray. But "Qibla" also represents the focal point of the aspirations and ideals of the Islamic community and in this sense there was no change in Qibla, as pointed out by a comtemporary Muslim scholar, since the House of God built by Abraham who founded the "Din" of Islam was, from the first, the intended center and unifying symbol of the Muslim ummah.

An idea that finds frequent expression in the Qur'an is that God will test the faith of all who profess to belive in God; for instance, Surah 21: *Al-Anbiya'*: 35, points out:

And We test you
By evil and by good
By way of trial.

It is of siginificance to note that according to the Qur'an, God designated the Ka'ba at Mecca as the Qibla in order to "test those who followed the Apostle." The Qur'an recognizes that this "change" would cause all "except . . . those guided by God" to turn their backs on the Islamic faith even though the appointment of the Qibla at the Ka'ba is a "favor" done to Muslims by God since that was the "Qibla to which thou wast used."

The question arises: why should the change in the direction for prayer be so "momentous" and why should it be regarded as a test of faith? It is hardly likely that Jerusalem was so important to the early Muslims that the instituting of the Qibla at the Ka'ba (which had been sacred to the Arabs since antiquity) would bring about a serious moral dilemma, nor does it seem probable that the problem of the coexistence of Muslims and Jews in Medina would have been much affected, either positively or negatively, by the change in the Muslim's Qibla. In my judgment, what the Qur'anic passage about the Qibla is pointing at is that the Muslim ummah has come - both historically and spiritually - to the end of one phase of development and is about to enter a new one, and that in order to enter the new phase an act of faith, of accepting the Will of God, is required, and this is where the test lies. (It is also of interest to observe here that at the time when the Ka'ba at Mecca was appointed the Qibla, it was in the possession of the pagan Quraish who were determined to wipe out Islam. It took an act of faith to believe that the Ka'ba would be purged of its profanities and delivered into the hands of Muslims to be re-sanctified by them).

From the beginning, Islam had been proud of its Abrahamic heritage and the early Muslims had turned their faces towards Jerusalem as they prayed in order to affirm their linkage with the People of the Book, just as the early Christians had insisted upon their connection with Israel. However, with the establishment of the first Islamic Society in Medina came the time and the necessity to stress not only the link of Islam with Abraham and Jerusalem but the link of Abraham to all humanity. Jerusalem - the Qibla of the People of the Book - had become associated with the exclusivism characteristic of many Jews and Christians. The former regarded themselves as the Chosen People, while the latter also made special claims to salvation through their belief in Jesus Christ. By turning the attention of the Muslim ummah from Jerusalem to the Qibla in Mecca, the Qur'an was, in fact, bringing about a profound change in perspective. The conflict underlying the need for this change was not localized antagonism between Muslims and Jews in Medina - as is frequently suggested by non-Muslim writers - but a much wider opposition between the principles of exclusivism and universalism.

Anyone who has read the Qur'an without bias is aware that Islam is truly universal in its ideals. In this context it is interesting to note that whilst the Old Testament frequently talks of the God of Abraham, Isaac and Jacob, the Qur'an never does. It describes Islam as the "Din" of Abraham and the other Prophets but does not describe God as the God of Abraham or the God of Muhammad. In Surah Fatiha, the opening chapter of the Qur'an, God is described as "Rabb al-'alamin" - God of all the peoples and universes. The Qur'an testifies that the message it contains is meant for all creatures, for instance:

25[1] Blessed is He Who
Sent down the Criterion (Qur'an)
To His Servant, that it
May be an admonition
To all creatures.

36[69] This is no less than
A Message to (all)
The Worlds.
70 That it may give admonition
To any (who are) alive,
And that the charge
May be proved against those
Who reject (Truth).

38[87] This is no less than
A Message to (all)
The Worlds.

81[27] Verily this is no less
Than a Message
To (all) the Worlds:
28 (With profit) to whoever
Among you wills
To go straight.

The non-exclusive spirit of Islam also comes through the oft-repeated teaching of the Qur'an contained in verses such as the following:

2[62] Those who believe (in the Qur'an)
And those who follow the Jewish (scriptures),
And the Christians and the Sabians.
And who believe in God
And the Last Day,
And work righteousness,
Shall have their reward
With their Lord; on them
Shall be no fear, nor shall they grieve.

2[111] And they say: "None
Shall enter Paradise unless
He be a Jew or a Christian."
Those are their (vain) desires.
Say: Produce your proof
If ye are truthful.
112 Nay, - whoever submits
His whole self to God
And is a doer of good, -
He will get his reward
With his Lord;
On such shall be no fear,
Nor shall they grieve.

2[268] And God careth for all
And He knoweth all things.
2[281] And fear the Day
When ye shall be
Brought back to God
Then shall every soul
Be paid what it earned,
And none shall be
Dealt with unjustly.

4[95] Unto all (in Faith)
Hath God promised good.

5[20] (Both) the Jews and the Christians
Say "We are Sons
Of God, and His beloved."
Say, Why then doth he
Punish you for your sins?
Nay, ye are but men, -
Of the men He hath created:
He forgiveth whom He pleaseth,
And to God belongeth
The dominion of heavens
And the earth, and all
That is between:
And unto Him
Is the final goal (of all).

5[72] Those who believe (in the Qur'an)
Those who follow the Jewish (scriptures),
And the Sabians and the Christians, -
Any who believe in God
And the Last Day
And work righteousness, -
On them shall be no fear,
Nor shall they grieve.

16[89] One day We shall raise
From all peoples a witness.

To Muslims, Abraham is an embodiment of the universalism implicit in Islam and it is the Abrahamic spirit which enables Muslims to become "witnesses for humanity"

22[78] And strive in his Cause
As ye ought to strive,
(With sincerity and under discipline).
He has chosen you, and has
Imposed no difficulties on you
In religion; it is the cult of your father Abraham.
It is he who named
You Muslims, both before
And in this (Revelation);

That the Apostle may be
A witness for you, and ye
Be witnesses for mankind.

It is of importance to note that the Qur'anic verses which refer to the Ka'ba (which Abraham built) relate the Ka'ba to all humanity and not to any specific group of people:

2[125] Remember We made the house
A place of Assembly for men
And a place of safety;
And take ye the Station
Of Abraham as a place
Of prayer; and We covenanted
With Abraham and Isma'il,
That they should sanctify
My House for those who
Compass it round, or use it
As a retreat, or bow, or
Prostrate themselves (therein
In prayer)

3[96] The first house (of worship)
Appointed for men
Was that at Bakka:
Full of blessing
And of guidance
For all kinds of beings.

[97] In it are Signs
Manifest; (for example),
The Station of Abraham;
Whoever enters it
Attains security;
Pilgrimage thereto is a duty
Men owe to God -
Those who can afford
The journey; but if any
Deny faith, God stands not
In need of any of His creatures.

5[100] God made the Ka'ba,
The Sacred House, an asylum
Of security for men, as
Also the Sacred Months,
The animals of offerings,
And the garlands that mark them:
That ye may know
That God hath knowledge
Of what is in the heavens
And on earth and that God
Is well acquainted
With all things.

In my judgment, on the basis of the above-mentioned verses, a clear case can be made out for making Mecca an open city. I would like to ask the government of Saudi Arabia how access to Mecca can be denied to non-Muslims in view of the unambiguous Qur'anic statements asserting that the Ka'ba is a sanctuary for all humankind.

Having reflected upon the significance of Hagar and Abraham in the Islamic tradition, it is important to say a few words about he "sacrifice" of their son Ishmael. Here it is of interest to note that while in the Jewish and Christian traditions the son Abraham was about to sacrifice was Isaac, in the Islamic tradition it was Ishmael. From the perspective of the latter, since the son whom God commanded Abraham to sacrifice was his "only" son, the son in question had to be Ishmael who was Abraham's first son. The former traditions have ignored Ishmael in favor of Isaac because they do not accord to Hagar the same status of being Abraham's "wife" as they do to Sarah. The Islamic tradition does not, however, distinguish between the status of Hagar and Sarah, or Ishmael and Isaac.

The Qur'anic narrative which begins with a reference to the time when Abraham prayed for a son, reads as follows:

37:100 (Abraham prayed)
"O my Lord! grant me
A righteous (son)!"

101 So We gave him
The good news
Of a boy ready
To suffer and forbear.

102 Then, when (the son)
Reached (the age of)
(Serious) work with him,
He said: "O my son!
I see in vision
That I offer thee in sacrifice:
Now see what is
Thy view!" (The son) said:
"O my father! Do
As thou art commanded:
Thou will find me,
If Allah so wills one
Practicing patience and constancy!"

103 So when they had both
Submitted their wills (to Allah),
And he had laid him
Prostrate on his forehead
(For sacrifice),

104 We called out to him,
"O Abraham!

105 Thou hast already fulfilled
Thy vision!" - thus indeed
Do we reward
Those who do right.

106 For this was obviously
A trial -

107 And We ransomed him
With a momentous sacrifice

108 And We left (this blessing)
For him among generations
(To come) in later times.

109 "Peace and salutation
To Abraham!"

110 Thus indeed do We reward
Those who do right

111 For he was one
Of Our believing Servants.

It is of interest to note that in the above-cited narrative the "son" is not named. However, unlike Isaac in the Biblical narrative, the son in this story does know that God had commanded his father to sacrifice him. The Qur'anic narrative, therefore, lacks the suspense of disclosure found in the Biblical story. What this narrative stresses is the obedience to God of both Abraham and Ishmael who symbolize what it means to be "Muslim". While Abraham and Ishmael do not show the slightest hesitation in accepting God's command, God also does not show any hesitation in offering immediate ransom for the son. Thus, while the story illustrates the faith of Abraham and Ishmael, it also shows the mercy and compassion of God toward those who remain steadfast in their resolve to live and die in accordance with the will and pleasure of God. That one cannot enter Paradise without being tested is clearly stated in the Qur'an which also points out that, oftentimes, what we have - particularly our children and material possessions - distract us from our highest goals. The test put to Abraham and Ishmael was the most difficult kind imaginable. That they came through it shows that it is possible for "Muslims" to overcome the bondage of attachment to all that is not-God.

Abraham's struggle against various forms of idolatry in his quest for the Ultimate are highlighted in the Qur'an. This struggle ranges from rejection of natural phenomena such as the stars, moon and sun[16] as God, to his dissociation from his idol-worshipping father once he realized that his father was an enemy of God.[17] The challenge of idolatry did not exist only at the time of Abraham. Idolatry exists today in subtler forms which pervade virtually every aspect of the consciousness of contemporary humanity. The struggle of Abraham, first to find God, and then to remain faithful to God, in the face of powerful material distractions and obstructions as well as natural affections and inclinations, is, thus, profoundly relevant to us.

The story of Abraham, Hagar and Ishmael which is commemorated and celebrated by Muslims on the occasion of 'Eid al'Adha remains an undying source of strength and courage, hope and faith, not only for Muslims but also for Jews, Christians and others who can understand its symbolism and what it can mean for those who consider themselves seekers and servants of God.

Notes

1. Gibb, H.A.R. and Kramers, J.H. (Editors), *Shorter Encyclopedia of Islam*, E.J. Brill, Leiden, 1953, p. 156.
2. *Ibid.*
3. *Ibid.*
4. *Ibid.*
5. Sometimes this term is used to mean "sajdah" or the act of prostration in prayer, and sometimes it is applied to the middle part ot the whole salat. To say that salat consists of so many "rak'as" means "that the introductory rites which precede the first 'kira'a' and those which follow the second 'sudjud' need occur only once in the salat in question, while, on the other hand, the ceremonies in between are repeated so many times." (*Ibid.* p. 494)
6. *Ibid.*, p. 161.
7. *Ibid.*, pp. 416-417.
8. *Ibid.* p. 156.
9. Khan, Muhammad Muhsin, translation of *Sahih Al-Bukhari*, Lahore, Kazi Publications, 1983, Volume IV, pp. 372-376. A partial reference to the story is made in the preceding hadi*th* (Number 582) which reads:

   Narrated Ibn 'Abbas: The Prophet said, "May Allah bestow His Mercy on the mother of Ishmael! Had she not hastened (to fill her water-skin with water from the Zam-zam well), Zam-zam would have been a stream flowing on the surface of the earth." Ibn 'Abbas further added, "(The Prophet) Abraham brought Ishmael and his mother (to Mecca) and she was suckling Ishmael, and she had a water-skin with her." (p. 372)
10. The fact that Hagar is referred to as "Ishmael's mother" or as "the mother of Ishmael" should not be interpreted to mean that Hagar's identity as a person/woman is being subsumed in her identity as a mother, or that she is seen as nothing more than the mother of a son. In Arab culture, it is customary to refer not only to women but also to men as being "mother" or "father" of "so-and-so". No gender-discrimination is, thus, implied by this form of address.
11. This hadi*th* reads as follows:

    Narrated Ibn 'Abbas: "When Abraham had differences with his wife (because of her jealousy of Hagar, Ishmael's mother), he took Ishmael and his mother and went away. They had a water-skin with them containing some water, Ishmael's mother used to drink water from the water-skin so that her milk would increase for her child. When Abraham reached Mecca, he made her sit under a tree and afterwards returned home. Ishmael's mother followed him, and when they reached Kada' she called him from behind, 'O Abraham! To whom are you leaving us?' He replied '(I am leaving you) to Allah's (Care)! 'She said, 'I am satisfied to be with Allah.' She returned to her place and started drinking water from the water-skin, and her milk increased for her child. When the water had all been used up, she said to herself, 'I'd better go and look so that I may see somebody.' She ascended the Safa mountain and looked, hoping to see somebody, but in vain. When she came down to the valley, she ran till she reached the Marwa mountain. She ran to and fro (between the two mountains) many times. Then she said to herself, 'I'd better go and see the state of the child,' she went and found it in a state of one on the point of dying. She could not endure to watch it dying and said (to herself), 'If I go and look, I may find somebody,' She went and ascended the Safa mountain and looked for a long while but could not find anybody. Thus she completed seven rounds (of running) between Safa and Marwa. Again she said (to herself), "I'd better go and see the state of the child.' But suddenly she heard a voice, and she said to that strange voice, 'Help us if you can offer any help.' Lo! It was Gabriel (who made the voice). Gabriel hit the earth with his heel like this (Ibn 'Abbas hit the earth with his heel to illustrate it), and so the water gushed out. Ishmael's mother was astonished and started digging. (Abu Al-Qasim i.e., the Prophet, said, 'If she had left the water, i.e., flow naturally without her intervention, it would have been flowing on the surface of the earth') Ishmael's mother started drinking from the water and her milk increased for her child. Afterwards some people of the tribe of Jurhum, while passing through the bottom of the valley, saw some birds, and that astonished them, and they said, 'Birds can only be found at a place where there is water.' They sent a messenger who searched the place and found the water, and returned to inform them about it. Then they all went to her and said, 'O Ishmael's mother! Will you allow us to be with you (or dwell with you?)' (And thus they stayed there.) Later on her boy reached the age of puberty and married a lady from them. Then an idea occurred to Abraham which he disclosed to his wife (Sarah), I want to call on my dependents I left (at Mecca). When he went there, he greeted (Ishmael's wife) and said, 'Where is Ishmael?' She replied, 'He has gone out hunting.' Abraham said (to her), 'When he comes, tell him to change the threshold of his gate.' When he came, she told him the same whereupon Ishmael said to her, 'You are the threshold, so go to your family (i.e., you are divorced).

(*Translator's footnote reads: "This very stone is still preserved in the Sacred Mosque in Mecca and is situated between the Ka'ba and Zam-zam, and one can see the footmarks of Abraham over it.")

12. In this context, the following observation taken from *Tafsiru'l Baizawi*, p. 424, quoted by T.P. Hughes in *A Dictionary of Islam*, Lahore: Premier Book House originally printed in 1885, is interesting: "When the tribe of Jurhum saw that there was water in that place, they said to Hagar, 'If you will share with us the water of this spring, we will share with you the milk of our herds', and from that time Mekkah became a place of importance." (p. 154)
13. As, for instance, Surah 4: *An-Nisa'*: 95, 97-100, and Surah 16: *An-Nahl*:, 41.
14. Parwez, G.A. *Lughat-ul-Qur'an*, Idara Tulu'-e-Islam, Lahore, 1960, Volume II, pp. 556-557.
15. All the translations of the Qur'anic passages cited below are taken from *The Holy Qur'an*, Translation and Commentary by 'Abdullah Yusuf 'Ali, Amana Corporation, Brentwood, Maryland, 1989.
16. For instance, see *The Qur'an*, Surah 6: *Al-An'am*: 75-82, Surah 21: *Al-Anbia'*: 51-70.
17. For instance, see *The Qur'an*, Surah 6: *Al-An'am*: 74, Surah 9: *At-Taubah*: 114, Surah 19: *Maryam*: 42-47.

List of Contributors

1. Dr. Willem A. Bijlefeld was the Editor of *The Muslim World* and Professor of Theology and Christian-Muslim Relations, until his retirement, at Hartford Theological Seminary, Hartford, Connecticut.
2. Prof. Michael E. Dyson is Assistant Professor of American Civilization and Afro-American Studies at Brown University, Providence, Rhode Island.
3. Dr. Ernest Hamilton, former Editor of *The Muslim World*, is Researcher attached to the Center for Jewish-Christian Studies, Chicago.
4. Dr. Riffat Hassan is Professor of Religious Studies at the University of Louisville, Louisville, Kentucky.
5. Dr. André LaCocque, the editor of this volume, is Professor of Hebrew Scriptures and Director of the Center for Jewish-Christian Studies, at the Chicago Theological Seminary, Chicago.
6. Dr. Jon D. Levenson is Professor of Judaic Studies at Harvard University Harvard, Cambridge, Massachusetts.
7. Dr. John T. Pawlikowski, O.S.M., is Professor of Ethics at Catholic Theological Union, Chicago.
8. Dr. Fazlur Rahman was Professor of Islamic Thought at the University of Chicago from 1969-1986.
9. Dr. Rolf Rendtorff is Professor Emeritus of Old Testament Studies at the University of Heidelberg, Heidelberg, Germany.
10. Dr. Byron L. Sherwin is Vice-President for Academic Affairs and Professor of Jewish Philosophy and Mysticism at Spertus College of Judaica, Chicago.